LOCAL FIRST

Development for the twenty-first century

LOCAL FIRST

Development for the twenty-first century

Edited by Kate McGuinness

PEACE DIRECT
SUPPORTING LOCAL ACTION AGAINST CONFLICT

Published in 2012 by Peace Direct,
Development House, 56-64 Leonard Street,
London EC2A 4LT. Registered charity 1123241.

Further information at www.peacedirect.org
or at www.localfirst.org.uk.

ISBN 978-0-9552419-2-5.

Printed by Marstan Press, Kent.

CONTENTS

'Success should not be measured by outputs or the amount of money spent, but by the ability of Afghan institutions to deliver services, the Afghan private sector to generate jobs, and Afghan civil society to provide avenues for citizens to hold their governments accountable.'

– US SENATE COMMITTEE ON FOREIGN RELATIONS

'What was useful in Kenya was that the internationals provided the pressure on the opponents – and the space – for them to come to an agreement. It ceased to be useful when the internationals began to specify what that agreement should be.'

– KENYAN PEACEBUILDER DEKHA IBRAHIM ABDI

Editor's note

The World Bank's *World Development Report 2011* reveals that 1.5 billion people live in countries affected by fragility, conflict or large-scale, organised criminal violence. The report goes on to state:

> *'No low-income fragile or conflict-affected country has yet achieved a single Millenium Development Goal. People in fragile and conflict-affected states are more than twice as likely to be undernourished as those in other developing countries, more than three times as likely to be unable to send their children to school, twice as likely to see their children die before age five, and more than twice as likely to lack clean water. On average, a country that experienced major violence over the period from 1981 to 2005 has a poverty rate 21 percentage points higher than a country that saw no violence' (World Development Report 2011: 5).*

Moreover, an average developing country caught up in protracted conflict loses roughly 30 years of GDP growth.

Such disturbing data provides an impetus for this collection of case studies, the objective of which is to showcase successful examples of change-related activities that originate at the local level and have scaled up to create a widespread, sustainable impact. More to the point, it is local people living with these facts on the ground, and working tirelessly to transform them for the better, who inform and inspire this book. As the global community nears the end of the timeframe for achieving the Millennium Development Goals in 2015, and moves forward in the direction of a post-Busan world development agenda, it is increasingly clear there is room for improvement. But this is not news. It has been known for some time – not least by those 1.5 billion people who live day in and day out with the realities of profound insecurity, poverty and bad governance.

Methodologically, the selection of these case studies exemplifies a primary tenet of the Local First approach: start from where you are, look at available resources and take it from there. In particular, these case studies were chosen because they represent compelling examples of large-scale activities that engage local capacity to the fullest extent. Each of these case studies was commissioned by

Carolyn Hayman of Peace Direct, who plays a leading role in the Local First campaign. Hence, they are tipped in favour of peacebuilding, with three of the six case studies focused on such issues. From a pragmatic perspective, this is what Peace Direct knows best, so it made sense to start from there. Reflecting the often organic approach to scaling up via networks and relationship building at the local level and moving upward and outward to reach ever broader constituencies, these case studies were also the result of a similar process of networking and relationship building related to activating the Local First campaign.

The sequence of the case studies in this collection moves from war to peace, as this may be metaphorically interpreted. The first two case studies focus on initiatives related to the challenges of disarmament, demobilisation and reintegration in the Democratic Republic of Congo and Burundi. The third case study discusses small and light weapons collection in post-conflict Mozambique. Shifting gears to the context of good governance, the fourth case study explains a judicial reform process in Cambodia and the fifth presents a model for local accountability in Timor Leste. Signalling a transition to the field of development, the sixth and final case study addresses the issue of local procurement in Afghanistan. The End Note in this volume situates the Local First approach in relation to a broader controversy about the roles of inside versus outside interveners, concluding that Local First constitutes a valuable middle ground that moves this long-standing debate to a new terrain. In one way or another, all of the topics herein reflect key aspects of the New Deal for Engagement in Fragile States.[1] They also represent an important degree of geographical diversity in post-conflict states.

Nonetheless, it is obvious that this volume does not aim to offer a comprehensive overview of local initiatives related to security, governance and development in post-conflict countries. Rather, they are intended to contribute to increasing the evidence base for local action, in particular by demonstrating that it can be effective on a large scale. These case studies further serve to share knowledge about best practice in partnerships between local and outside

---

1 *The New Deal identifies five peacebuilding and state-building goals: 1) legitimate politics; 2) security; 3) justice; 4) economic foundations; and 5) revenues and services managed accountably and ensuring fair service delivery. For the full text, see: http://www. oecd.org/international%20dialogue/49151944.pdf.*

actors. As Hayman makes clear, Local First is by no means 'local only'. Importantly, this collection also offers a launch pad for the Local First campaign, with all of the authors working for and with organisations that have a strong commitment to the Local First approach. Hayman outlines the central precepts of the Local First approach in the Introduction to this book.

Among the gaps that show up in this unavoidably limited collection of examples, one bears special mention. Although there are now unprecedented levels of worldwide attention to women's involvement in peacebuilding, a gender-specific case study is not included here. Despite the high degree of interest, there is still limited research and concrete evidence about women's engagement at the local or micro level and how this can be scaled up. Fortunately, however, a recent publication works to remedy this imbalance. Just as this volume seeks to contribute to the evidence base that documents the impact and effect of local action, *From the Ground Up* helps to address the absence of information about the roles women play in peacebuilding at the local level. As such, it can be considered complementary to the Local First initiative.

Each of the case studies here begins with a short description of the context from which the project in question emerged, paying specific attention to the political and security challenges in the country where it is based. They also define the need or problem that prompted the local response, as well as identify the intended project beneficiaries. The bulk of each case study then focuses on the approach that the organisation adopted, how this evolved, available organisational resources and some background information about the organisation and its founders. Here is where these stories come to life, drawing on anecdotes, interview quotes and testimonial evidence from those who were involved in the project in some way – staff, participants, beneficiaries, community members, government actors and funders.

The case studies move on to briefly discuss project partnerships and how they worked, and then address issues related to evaluation, effectiveness and cost-effectiveness. Some of them reference comparative data (where relevant and available) from internationally led interventions in the same general area of work. Finally, the case studies offer lessons learnt, conclusions and recommendations oriented to establishing more effective practice on the ground.

These examples of local action comprise a mix of qualitative and quantitative data, with emphasis on the former. In general, data is drawn from face-to-face interviews with key informants and staff (along with follow-up correspondence), focus group discussions, secondary interview material, a variety of organisational reports, including both internal and external evaluations, as well as related publications, statistical documentation and scholarly material. References appear at the end of each chapter. Appendices with biographical notes, brief organisational profiles and contact details are included at the end of the book.

I wish to thank Carolyn Hayman and Jonathan Lorie of Peace Direct for their valuable input and feedback on all of the case studies. I also extend many thanks to all of the authors and their organisational counterparts. They were a pleasure to work with, graciously responding to my queries for clarification and additional information with full cooperation and on a timely basis, despite the pressures of their own busy work lives.

These are powerful stories about how change can happen from the bottom up, growing to a large scale and having a far-reaching, sustainable impact. These are honest assessments of the challenges, limitations and failures in trying to do so. Above all, these are inspiring examples which offer cautious grounds for optimism that a better future could be built – provided local knowledge, experience and commitment are taken more seriously by the world at large.

Who decides how to do what? This is the crucial question that Local First raises.

Kate McGuinness, Berlin, 3 March 2012

References

ActionAid, Institute of Development Studies, Womankind Worldwide. *From the Ground Up: Women's Roles in Local Peacebuilding in Afghanistan, Liberia, Nepal, Pakistan and Sierra Leone*. London: ActionAid, Institute of Development Studies, Womankind Worldwide, 2012.

World Bank. *World Development Report 2011*. New York: World Bank, 2011.

Introduction
Local First – a proposal for development in the twenty-first century

by Carolyn Hayman [1]

Local First is a development approach that looks first for the capacity within countries before bringing in external expertise and resources, recognises that much of this capacity is found outside central government, and understands that local people need to lead their own development.

Summary

It's hard to imagine a simpler or more commonsense idea – that development initiatives should support and amplify existing local activity, including civil society, private sector suppliers and government, rather than starting from scratch with goods and services from outside; and that development initiatives should be judged to a significant degree on the extent to which they leave local organisations stronger and more capable than at the outset.

Local First implies that outsiders engage with local perceptions of problems and solutions, and seek out and build on pockets of effectiveness wherever they are found. Doing so can make maximum use of local knowledge, reinforce self-help and self-reliance, and offer encouragement and self-confidence to local organisations. Local First is not an argument for or against aid. Instead, it is based on the idea that aid should consciously and assertively assist countries to move to self-reliance through a self-help process that is locally led and determined.

1 *The author wishes to thank Building Markets, CEDAC, Centre Résolution Conflits, FOMICRES, International Bridges to Justice, and Integrity Action (formerly known as Tiri), as well as many others, for input and feedback on earlier drafts of this chapter.*

13

Putting Local First into practice requires rethinking assumptions about impact, developing new approaches to finding local capacity, and shaping partnerships that work with local organisations on an equal footing. In short, the way that outsiders work with local organisations, whether state or non-state, matters. Crucial to the Local First agenda is the difference between three styles of working:

1. **Locally led,** where the local partner sets priorities and formulates the approach, and the outside agency provides, for example, resources and connections to organisations working in similar ways for mutual learning and support.

2. **Locally owned,** where the approach comes from outside but there is a determined effort to transplant ownership of the work to a legitimate local organisation that over time can transform the programme into one that is locally led.

3. **Locally delivered,** where the approach comes from outside and a local organisation is selected to implement it, without having been involved in setting the priorities or the approach, and where there is no transfer of ownership.

Across this spectrum of possible styles of engagement with local organisations, Local First is most closely identified with the first, a locally led approach.[2] Assuming that the second, locally owned, is eventually locally led, Local First can also be linked to this approach. The third, locally delivered, is not regarded as part of Local First. Rather, this defines a more typical or traditional approach to development that is part and parcel of the problem Local First is designed to address.

Local First is not a wholly novel approach and there are many encouraging examples where it has been put into practice. However, most aid is still heavily influenced in its deployment by outside agencies. This is also the case with peacebuilding. The case studies in this book illustrate the capacity for concerted social and political action that exists in the categories defined by the World Bank as priorities in post-conflict countries – security, justice and livelihoods. But Local First is applicable across the whole of the development field, including humanitarian assistance (Section I).[3]

Local First makes sense for the following reasons. Local direction encourages self-help and discourages dependency. Local

---

2 Hereafter, 'locally led' and 'Local First' represent equivalent terms.
3 Sections referred to in this Summary correspond to relevant parts of the Introduction.

procurement builds the economy and enables self-reliance. Locally led interventions are more likely to be relevant and sustainable. As these case studies illustrate, they can also be large-scale. Intuitively, they should be more cost-effective as well.[4] Ultimately, however, Local First aims for broad economic impact (job creation, skills development, poverty reduction, economic development, and so on) rather than cost savings alone (Section II).

Thorny issues remain regarding the impact of external funding on the legitimacy and effectiveness of local organisations. Anyone implementing a Local First approach needs to confront these practicalities. Although the academic literature on this is not encouraging, the case studies here suggest that locally led and locally owned initiatives can scale up without losing the voluntarism, relevance and accountability which are the foundations of their effectiveness, provided that their external partners support local leadership and facilitate meaningful local participation in decision-making processes (Section III).

Many organisations already claim to work with locals. So what is really different about Local First? 'How' matters, which is why Local First distinguishes between locally led, locally owned and locally implemented or delivered. What is critically important is to allow local ideas and perspectives to shape interventions (Section IV).

Some national governments may have reservations about the diversification of emphasis and the strengthening of the role of non-state actors that is implied by Local First. But they may feel compensated by a trade-off that gives more of the action to local organisations, including businesses, rather than outsiders. Local First also means that donors pay more attention to local context in their work with governments. Multilaterals and international non-governmental organisations (INGOs) will still play important roles, but need to rethink how they add value in a Local First world (Section V).

Recommendations to put Local First into practice include:

For donors:
- Enlarge the definition and role of capacity assessment, and ensure that the assessment includes the motivation and social accountability of organisations.

---

4 *Before this can be proven, research is needed to test this proposition.*

- Make a commitment to using external organisations as a last resort, not a first resort, and as supportive partners to local organisations, not as contractors.
- Identify a few sectors within which to experiment with a Local First approach and aim over time to direct an increasing percentage of funding within those sectors to locally led or locally owned programmes.
- Commit to long-term evaluations of impact, sustainability and value for money from locally led versus internationally led projects, using locally devised indicators that are relevant to the participants/beneficiaries.
- Enable and support structures that will allow local organisations to scale up their impact, and permit donor funds to be spread across a number of initiatives, recognising that the trend towards larger grants could otherwise work against the adoption of a Local First approach.
- Ensure that all evaluations include an assessment of the impact of the project on the growth or decline in local capacity, seeking to capture indirect as well as direct effects.

For INGOs:
- Evaluate in what ways organisational practice is locally led or locally owned and how this can be demonstrated.
- Set a goal to increase the Local First orientation of their work, and define how this increase can be demonstrated.
- Make a practice of seeking out local suppliers of goods and services, including audit, market research and evaluation.

For local NGOs:
- Seek funding and support on the organisation's own terms insofar as possible and resist being cast as delivery agents.
- Maintain the involvement of the wider community as volunteers and ensure that the organisation has a survival strategy in the absence of external funding.
- Remunerate paid staff in keeping with local wage rates.
- Seek to connect community-based activity with local and national government, as well as with the work of INGOs and multilaterals, in order to coordinate with and influence them.

I. What is Local First?

'Success should not be measured by outputs or the amount of money spent, but by the ability of Afghan institutions to deliver services, the Afghan private sector to generate jobs, and Afghan civil society to provide avenues for citizens to hold their governments accountable' *(US Senate, 2011).*

The idea of Local First is beginning to emerge in the academic literature on development, as is well expressed by Shivakumar:

'Development is always a local phenomenon where local refers to the relevant problem area. Human development and economic progress are rooted in the enhanced ability of individuals − brought together within specific contexts and in the light of some encountered collective action problem − to adapt by developing the institutional contexts needed to deal with their situation' (Shivakumar, 2005: 105).

Similarly, David Booth (2010: 4-5) summarises the success factors for public goods provision in Africa, identifying the three key conditions as:

- A coherent vision so that resources are allocated and incentives structured in ways that are mutually reinforcing not mutually undermining.
- Human resources components subject to effective top-down performance disciplines.
- Institutions enabling local collective action, which are locally anchored.

There are lots of examples where aid recognises the importance of local leadership or ownership. All too often, however, programmes are donor driven. The focus on assessing what the population needs is not matched by a similar assessment of what the population is already doing or could potentially do to meet those needs: so that the local capacity is never found or used. Or donors would genuinely prefer to work with local organisations, but do not see them having the scale that is required, and cannot tailor the scale of their grants to a level that local organisations could absorb. Donors also have inadequate infrastructure capacities when it comes to taking a Local First approach.

The case studies in this book illustrate successful examples where local organisations have been able to work at a scale that is significant in national terms, matching that of programmes run by INGOs or multilaterals, and in many cases in close partnership with both. They also show how local capacity in the private sector can be developed. As well as making the case for a greater use of local capacity, Local First suggests practical steps that would enable donors and INGOs to give local organisations a bigger role while meeting their own objectives.

The examples shown here are drawn from security, justice, livelihoods and accountability – all key issues in post-conflict countries, which is where these case studies are situated. In these settings, where trust is particularly important in order to create positive change, the role of local organisations is critical. But the same principle applies to all development work, perhaps nowhere more so than in the humanitarian field, where it can be challenging to make use of local capacity because of the twin needs of speed and scale.

Importantly, Local First does not mean 'local only', and the case studies illustrate a number of successful partnerships between local and outside organisations:

- In Mozambique, FOMICRES, an organisation of former child soldiers, worked with the South Africa Police Service to find and destroy weapons. FOMICRES had the local credibility to enter communities, whereas the South African Police Service had the technical skills to destroy weapons safely.
- In Cambodia, Legal Aid of Cambodia encouraged and supported International Bridges to Justice to help build a network of centres providing legal defence services to the poor.
- In Afghanistan, Building Markets used Western expertise and contacts to open up opportunities for Afghan businesses that led to procurement of US$1 billion over 6 years.
- In Timor Leste, a local accountability organisation, Luta Hamutuk, gained vital monitoring and reporting skills and the opportunity to link up with similar anti-corruption organisations in other post-conflict countries through working with Integrity Action (formerly known as Tiri).
- In DRC, the funding and support relationship between Centre Résolution Conflits and Peace Direct enabled CRC to apply its mediation skills to DDR and community development

programmes, and work in cooperation with MONUSCO to demobilise combatants.

- In Burundi, CEDAC worked with UNIFEM to establish a national structure of female ex-combatants and women associated with the armed forces, with committees at local, provincial and national level, which has become a permanent feature of CEDAC's network.

Local First also does not refer to sequencing in time. In certain contexts, particularly of hot conflict, an externally led intervention may provide the stability that allows local actors to be fully effective. In others, local organisations can help to prepare the ground for outside interventions to be effective. What is important, though, is to recognise the limitations of external interventions and the crucial need for local leadership. As the late peace activist Dekha Ibrahim Abdi commented on the external intervention in the post-election violence in Kenya, 'What was useful was that the internationals provided the pressure on the opponents – and the space – for them to come to an agreement. It ceased to be useful when they began to specify what that agreement should be.' [5]

If a key principle of Local First is to look for local capacity wherever it can be found, then the balance of funding going to central governments, on the one hand, and to other levels of government and all other public, private and not-for-profit organisations, on the other, needs to be reassessed.

There are good reasons why donors focus resources on central governments. Improving the quality of government is critically important. The capable accountable and responsive (CAR) state is rightly seen as one of the key drivers of development. Equally, considerations of equity mean that nationally led solutions, which can in theory be applied across the whole country, are preferred.

However, theory and reality part company in many cases. An overemphasis on quality of government at the expense of the value of civil society ignores the reality of how development happened in the early industrialised countries, where services were planned and delivered by many different organisations, in some cases for centuries, before governments adopted them as state responsibilities. For example, much of the UK education system, for both children and adults, was developed first by the churches and by associations of workers.

---

5 *Source: author's notes from a private presentation, May 2008.*

Social housing was invented by philanthropic organisations such as the Peabody Housing Trust. In the US, charitable institutions such as food banks, community organisations and private grant-making foundations play a significant role in alleviating poverty. All this applies where there arguably was, and still is, more state capacity and accountability than there is in many aid-receiving countries.

Clearly, then, capable, accountable and responsive organisations exist outside central government, as these case studies illustrate. A different set of examples would show how, even where central government as a whole is weak, there may be individual state or local officials, or ministries, that would repay investment in the spirit of Local First. The issue is not to privilege one sector over another, but to channel support to wherever conditions make it likely to be fruitful, and to encourage the building of state/civil society relations that will meet the first of Booth's conditions – a coherent vision so that different initiatives support, and do not undermine, one another.

One of the interesting and unexpected findings from these case studies is the way in which strong, non-partisan civil society organisations can influence the state and work with it to improve its own quality of governance and performance in meeting its obligations to its citizens. (See Box A.)

In addition, when citizens are involved in ensuring service delivery, or delivering services themselves as volunteers (eg, as focal points in the Timor Leste case study, or as members of the task forces in the DRC case study), their belief in their own power to create change grows. When they see an example of a service being delivered well, it raises their expectations of what can be expected from government.

Hence Local First argues that support to central governments for a small number of key functions, the choice of which will be context-specific, needs to be balanced by the encouragement of coordinated but pluralistic provision by a range of local organisations – NGOs, entrepreneurs, lower tiers of government and other forms of citizen association for the remainder. This is not a statement about the merits of large or small government, but recognition that capacity at central government level cannot be developed quickly across a wide range of functions. Building capacity from the ground up that can eventually be adopted for central or state-level funding is an alternative strategy which makes maximum use of local capacity and

---

Box A

In 2001, the Mozambican government created COPRECAL, the national small arms commission, with authority to coordinate all small arms and light weapons control activities. COPRECAL incorporates a strong presence from civil society, to the point where FOMICRES has represented the commission in international meetings in recent years (see chapter 3).

In 2012, the Cambodian Ministry of Justice signed a Memorandum of Understanding with International Bridges to Justice Cambodia. This promotes cooperation between the Ministry of Justice and IBJ Cambodia to create a sustainable legal aid system in Cambodia and as such is an important step towards building the structure of a strong and equitable justice sector. IBJ has also partnered with the Ministry of Justice to provide training for judges, prosecutors, defenders, police, military police and prison officials (see chapter 4).

In 2010, the Afghan Ministry of Defence started to post its tenders on the Building Markets' Tender Distribution Service, enabling them to reach a larger pool of contractors. Their success encouraged the Ministry of the Interior and Da Afghanistan Breshna Shirkat to follow suit (see chapter 6).

---

enables citizens to develop their accountability with organisations close to home.[6] Local First in procurement can also strengthen governments by increasing taxable revenues and reducing their costs of supply, as well as giving citizens greater economic opportunities.

The underlying assumption behind this proposal for Local First is that every country possesses its own leaders and leadership capacities – in civil society, the private sector and government – who can mobilise their fellow citizens to get things done. The case studies profile a handful of such leadership examples. The organisations supporting them could name many more. What differentiates these individuals and organisations is that they managed to secure

---

6 *For an example of how this could work in relation to land registration, see: How to Make Poverty History: the Central Role of Local Organisations in Meeting the MDGs. Tom Bigg and David Satterthwaite (eds.). London: International Institute for Environment and Development (IIED), 2005; http://pubs.iied.org/pdfs/11000IIED.pdf.*

resources (from a wide variety of sources) to scale up their work to the point where it made a significant impact without losing the qualities that made them effective in the first place.

II. Local First makes sense

There are four key reasons to advocate for and adopt the Local First approach. This is likewise an opportune moment to rethink the role of local actors and the valuable expertise and knowledge they possess, given the transition from the Millennium Development Goals to the post-Busan New Deal that will define how the international community engages with fragile and post-conflict states in future.

1. Fostering self-help
Aid is not development, although it can lead to development. Development happens when all the resources of a country are used to greatest effect – when the dynamism that exists is tapped into, and people practice self-help and mutual help, leading to self-reliance. Nowhere is this needed more than in post-conflict countries.

It is well known, but frequently forgotten, that very many public goods are provided informally, by informal or formal local organisations that fly below the radar of the aid system. They may not be operating along the same lines as an international organisation and they may not conform in every respect to international norms. This can present problems for funders, particularly around attitudes towards marginalised groups, including women. Among other things, these structures are rooted in the spirit of voluntarism, which can be one of the most precious assets a society has.[7] (See Box B.)

2. Relevance
If not carefully researched and planned, international interventions can seem irrelevant to the target population, ignoring pressing needs in favour of a currently fashionable intervention. This unfortunate observation is supported both by research and everyday experience

---

7 *Importantly, such structures can also be rooted in tradition or power relations, which can bring with them long entrenched patterns of hierarchy and exclusion that could serve to reinforce (not ameliorate) relations of social, cultural, political and economic inequality. However, this is not only a challenge for Local First, but for all development approaches.*

> **Box B**
>
> In an analysis of the HIV/AIDS issue, a Ugandan study for the Joint Learning Initiative on Children and AIDS at Harvard in 2007 revealed that the prevalence of community-level initiatives for children affected by HIV/AIDS was one per 1,300 people. A mapping exercise sponsored by UNICEF identified over 1,800 community-based organisations focused on orphans and vulnerable children in Malawi alone.
>
> *Source: Jennifer Lentfer, How Matters blog, 'Small is beautiful... Grants, that is'. See: http://www.how-matters.org/2011/01/13/ small-grants-part-2/.*

– of emergency housing that people will not live in, clinics built in the wrong place that end up as cowsheds and tractors sent as aid to mountainous terrain where they are unusable.

Even where the area of the intervention is one accorded high priority by citizens, the investment may be less effective than it might be by failing to build on what already exists. (See Box C.)

3. Sustainability

Keeping a development project going year in and year out is hard work. Projects and programmes that are not rooted in some aspect of the locality are unlikely to attract the necessary effort over time. So resources are wasted in creating projects that have a relatively short life span, and may crowd out work that has greater potential for sustainability, for example by draining away scarce talent.

The lack of sustainability has been acknowledged as a particular problem in the case of DDR programmes. Donor focus is too often on the disarmament and demobilisation phases, with time, resources and attention running out before the reintegration phase has been completed. (See Box D.)

Locally led approaches, such as those in the case studies of CRC and CEDAC, have the benefit of time. The implementing organisation remains at hand to support reintegration over the medium to long term. In addition, a locally led organisation knows that its wider credibility depends on the success of reintegration. The reintegration programme can more easily be adapted in the light of experience or changing conditions by a locally led organisation.

Box C

In East Timor, the attempted introduction of a formal justice system by UNTAET (United Nations Transitional Administration in East Timor) ignored the existence of traditional justice mechanisms that had widespread support, with 94 per cent of the population stating their confidence in community-based justice systems. In the words of Chopra, Ranheim and Nixon (2011: 120):

'The lack of acknowledgement of local structures has proved to be a general problem with post-Cold War international interventions. Most of these more complex "second generation" operations have paid little attention to traditional power structures at the grassroots level, assuming a complete blank slate and a vacuum of power. But quite the opposite is usually the case: the population relies even more strongly on its local authority structure, for this is often all that remains after the destruction of the state apparatus or the withdrawal of a government.'

---

4. Cost effectiveness

The potential waste of resources that can result from ignoring local perspectives is summed up in the observation by Min Shahi, director of a mediation organisation in Nepal, who comments, '$100 that I can use with my own discretion is worth $100,000 dollars to deliver a donor's programme.' [8]

Intuitively, local delivery should be more cost-effective than using external, often highly paid, experts from multilaterals, INGOs or the private sector. In the case of local procurement, there are clear cases of cost saving – for example, the US military reduced its bill for drinking water in Afghanistan from US$58 million per year to US$7.2 million per year by switching to an Afghan supplier.

However, in the security sector examples, comparisons are much more difficult, as one of two issues usually complicates calculations:

- Either local organisations and internationals are working in partnership and it is impossible to unpick the value that each contributes to the end result.
- Or local organisations are doing something that no international organisation would be able to do.

---

8 *Interview conducted with Min Shahi, Director, KIRDARC, Nepal in June 2008.*

> ## Box D
>
> As Nelson Alusala (2011: vii) asserts, 'Experience shows that the design of reintegration programmes should, as a matter of priority, include a clear understanding of the social, cultural, economic and political dynamics of both ex-combatants and the recipient communities. An understanding of these aspects should inform the planning of a reintegration programme and hence its sustainability. More often, however, DDR programmes have been designed with little or no consideration for either ex-combatants or the communities they are to reintegrated into. In many cases, donor communities are more concerned about fundraising for the DDR kitty and less about the programming of the reintegration process. By the time the reintegration stage is reached, the funds are usually exhausted, or donor fatigue will have set in, thereby crippling the realization of the most critical element of the DDR process.'

It appears, for example, that Centre Résolution Conflits was able to reintegrate a former combatant for US$153 compared with figures of US$300-750 for large-scale international DDR programmes in DRC (Gillhespy and Hayman, 2011: 28). However, a detailed comparison would be needed to assess whether comparable overhead costs were included, and the extent to which support from other organisations was material (eg, FAO provided seeds to CRC).

In local procurement, the picture is equally mixed. The Building Markets case study demonstrates clear savings in some cases, but also shows how producers in neighbouring countries such as Pakistan, working at a much larger scale and with a longer history, could undercut Afghan producers of boots. The 'infant industry' case for protection may be relevant here (see chapter 6).

Hence a recommendation is that longitudinal comparative studies be commissioned in a number of different fields in order to test the relative cost-effectiveness, effectiveness and longevity of locally led or locally owned versus externally driven interventions. Longevity is particularly important, as even projects that show success at one moment in time, such as the Afghan supplier of boots to the US military, can founder when conditions change (see chapter 6).

The cost savings that can accrue as a result of the Local First approach are obviously important. However, it is equally important to have a much broader perspective that includes building sustainable markets and local economies, job creation, skills development, business management capacities and so on. In other words, cost savings do not always equate to best value, if best value is understood to encompass comprehensive economic impact. In fact, cost savings can be false positives, especially if other economic advantages and livelihood opportunities are lost in the process, such as employment for vulnerable or marginalised groups.[9]

III. Local First raises practical issues

A Local First approach is messy. It implies using capacity wherever it can be found – whether in NGOs and community-based organisations, professional associations, local or state government, traditional justice systems, faith organisations, as well as central government. Some of these organisations have a long history of operating on a large scale – for example, at one point the Catholic Church in DRC had educated a significant proportion of the country's population. The church also played a significant role in Mozambique's weapons collection programme, through FOMICRES' partnership with the Christian Council of Mozambique.

In Cambodia, lawyers helped to build up the network of legal aid centres, and in Timor Leste, Luta Hamatuk works with local police, local government and the chiefs of sectoral offices, such as health and education. In DRC, the task forces that help to identify and then prevent conflict flashpoints are drawn from the military, local government and the churches, as well as former militia members.

Three of the most important practical issues that confront a Local First approach include:

1. Accountability and legitimacy
Any organisation receiving public funds needs to be accountable, both to the source of the funds and to the beneficiaries/participants in the public good that is being provided. Accountability can take many forms, and a recent paper has argued for 'watchdogs not

---

9 *The author wishes to acknowledge Claire Schouten (Integrity Action) and Ainsley Butler (Building Markets) for their insights and contribution to developing this distinction between cost savings and economic impact.*

widgets' – in other words, that accountability mechanisms should be assessed in terms of their encouragement of engagement, not whether they follow a particular methodology (see Joshi and Houtzager, 2012).

In general, social structures that have stood the test of time, which engage significant amounts of voluntary effort and which deliver public goods effectively, are likely to be widely accepted as legitimate. They may have significant defects, but the risks involved in replacing them with more formal voluntary association structures seem considerable, in terms of 'abuse of power, distortion due to "problem seeking" social division, increasing inequality and materialistic motivations, and the promotion of corruption and clientelism among leaders' (Booth, 2010: 26).

In an insightful examination of why external funding often produces these negative side effects, Bano (2012) explains the nature of the essential contract in an informal organisation as being between initiators and followers. Followers look to initiators, who made sacrifices to take up their role, as an indication of commitment to non-material motivations. It is this relationship that confers legitimacy.

2. Scale and professionalisation

There are potentially many organisations in a low income country that are capable of delivering effectively and could scale up if resources were made available. However, as mentioned above, there are risks in bringing in external funds to achieve this; eg, in terms of the distortion of incentives and the discouragement of voluntary effort. Academic research tends to suggest that this route to scaling up loses precisely the qualities that made them effective in the first place, or indeed can actually destroy the organisation, by substituting material for non-material incentives.

However, the case studies here suggest that these difficulties can be overcome, and that organisations can grow considerably in scale, as well as employ a team of paid staff, without losing their ability to mobilise voluntary effort. Intuitively, this seems to be related to the way that they engaged with outside funders:

- They were pre-existing organisations, which had been created in response to a need, not to a funding opportunity.
- The organisations began with a voluntary self-help ethos.
- They sought funding or partnership (or in the case of IBJ

Cambodia, where the local director moved from his previous position, a job) on their own terms.
- They kept the rewards to paid staff in line with local levels.

These empirical findings line up with Bano's (2012: chapter 5) recommendations about how to avoid destroying organisations through external funding:
- Do not pay high salaries to initiators: these sap both their own motivation and that of their followers.
- Fund material activities that benefit the whole organisation.
- Monitor performance in terms of members' satisfaction and engagement.
- Be willing to work with organisations on equal terms, listening to their perspectives and approaches to development.
- Adjust incentives over time as the work develops.

3. Challenges in choosing organisations to work with

Section VI suggests ways to broaden the fields of possible development partners and assess their capacity. Issues will arise in terms of language. Will effective organisations be ruled out because they do not speak the donor's language? There is also a risk of creating tensions among local partners by selecting one organisation over another. Capacity assessments need to go beyond the submission of formal proposals and might usefully reflect the way that in-country supporters assess organisations, for example, through:
- Direct contact with the organisation's work.
- Recommendations from trusted people or networks.
- Longevity of the organisation and its work in that field.
- Level of commitment of the initiators.

Such an assessment approach requires resources and a long-term connection with the field, either through placing staff in the field, by building up networks that can be relied upon to channel funds to effective organisations or by using intermediaries that have demonstrated their commitment to a Local First approach.

IV. Everyone works with locals...

Every organisation – INGO, multilateral or donor – claims that they work with locals. But seemingly minor or subtle differences in how they work with locals matter enormously. Here are some tests to distinguish the three possible approaches:

Is it locally led?
- Does the planned activity grow organically out of the local organisation's experience and understanding of the situation, in terms of both need and capacity?
- Can it be delivered making substantial use of the skills and knowledge that already exist?
- Has the activity been prioritised by the local organisation?
- Is the local organisation able to decide where the activity is most needed and how to carry it out?
- Is there an effective, possibly informal, mechanism for accountability to the local population, which could include market forces?

Is it locally owned?
- Has the appropriateness of the idea to the local situation been thoroughly tested?
- Has widespread local support for the idea been generated?
- Are there local organisations with a commitment to taking over responsibility for running the project over time?
- Does project evaluation include the transfer of responsibility?
- Does the project mobilise local voluntary effort?
- Does the initiator of the project have an exit plan in terms of management responsibility?
- Is there an effective, possibly informal, mechanism for accountability to the local population, which could include market forces?

Is it locally implemented?
- Did the local organisation have little or no input into the choice of project and project design?
- Is the local component in the form of locally employed staff, who have little strategic decision-making authority?
- Were the priorities for the project and the criteria for success set by the funder and/or external initiator?
- Is the local organisation delivering the project showing commitment to it, for example by mobilising volunteer labour?

- Are per diems or other material incentives being paid to induce local participation?
- Does the project use an approach that has been successful elsewhere, but has not been validated in that country? [10]
- Does the project adopt external values, the salience of which among the target population has not been tested?

A project that is locally led has the potential to express to the highest degree the qualities of being capable, accountable and responsive. Rooted in the community's needs and capacities, it can respond to changing circumstances, capitalise on opportunities, and engender a sense of ownership, self-help and community solidarity. Of these case studies, Mozambique, Timor Leste, DRC and Burundi exemplify the locally led approach, although CEDAC in Burundi also works in local delivery mode.

Where projects are locally owned, the external organisation partners with one or more existing local organisations, pooling knowledge of what has worked elsewhere with the local organisation's understanding of the environment, and their connections and credibility. Sustained effort is made to transfer ownership and strategic direction over time to the local organisation, and to ensure that voluntary effort is mobilised. The case studies in Cambodia and Afghanistan work in this way.

All too often, though, local organisations are used simply to implement or deliver projects devised far away by donors and contracted to INGOs. Using local organisations simply as 'boots on the ground' is disempowering and high-risk, as it sidelines much of the spectrum of skills and experience that could be used. (See Box E.)

V. Will Local First be accepted by national governments? How will multilaterals add value using Local First approaches? What will this mean for INGOs?

Even if donor governments could be persuaded of the benefits of

---

10 *It is encouraging to see that guidance for one of DfID's grant programmes notes as a negative indicator 'reference to international experience as proof that the proposed intervention will work in the proposed project context without due consideration of the specific local conditions'. Source: http://www.dfid.gov.uk/Documents/funding/gpaf/GPAF-Impact-Concept-Notes-Key-strengths-Weaknesses.pdf.*

Box E

A local peacebuilding organisation had been promised a substantial grant from a Western government for its work on inter-religious harmony, in a country where the work was politically controversial. Long after the contract was due to be finalised, they received a series of conditions from the donor, which required them to change almost every aspect of the programme, including the participants at their meetings, the structure of the meetings and the words used. They were also required to reveal everything about the project to the head of the provincial government, as well as provide incentives to the government officials to make them more favourably inclined. As the project's success to date had depended on flying under the radar, they reluctantly turned down the funds, though these were badly needed.

---

a Local First approach, would recipient governments accept it? Would the trade-off of greater use of local capacity, and a greater role for recipient governments in shaping their own contribution, compensate for the possible loss of access to aid funds and the prestige that comes from deploying those funds? Can desire to provide better public goods be harnessed?

The enthusiasm for the post-Busan New Deal for building peaceful states suggests that the principle of involving civil society more closely in a coherent national plan for peacebuilding is gaining acceptance. A concerted effort to implement Local First will show where the reluctance is in recipient country governments, multilaterals and INGOs.

Multilaterals will continue to have a big role to play. As the case studies demonstrate, their access to resources, technical expertise and logistical capacity can be invaluable to their local partners. But they need to be genuinely doing things that could not be done by one or more local organisations (see Section VI below) and there needs to be far more rigorous scrutiny of the cost-effectiveness of working through multilaterals. Good examples of partnership need to be encouraged, for example the principle of co-design of projects with local partners, to try to ensure that the work is effective for local communities, as well as fitting within a larger programme.

Local First also represents a challenge for INGOs. There will certainly continue to be role for them, but it may be a changing one – less an implementer, deliverer of stand-alone capacity building programmes and conduit for donor funds, and more a discoverer and nurturer of local talent, with a very clear objective of enabling organisations to lead from the beginning, and to contribute their knowledge to the INGO and its other partners.

VI. Putting Local First into practice

The proposals in this paper present a paradox. They could be viewed as a small shift in the role of international intermediaries vis-a-vis local entities. Many donors and INGOs genuinely believe that their approach is Local First. But in fact they require a fundamental transfer of leadership and decision making from outsiders to insiders. The question is how to express this transfer in concrete actions?

Here are six suggestions for donors, three for INGOs and four for local organisations.

Suggestions for donors

Suggestion 1: Enlarge the definition and role of capacity assessment, and ensure that the assessment includes the motivation and social accountability of organisations.

No one could accuse donors and multilaterals of not taking capacity assessment seriously as a topic. There is a huge wealth of technical material on the subject (eg, see the body of work summarised in the UNDG Capacity Assessment Practice Note 2008). Despite this, the observation made almost 20 years ago in an analytical review for UNDP still has validity:

> 'Capacity development should not be equated with training, education and technology transfer. Attention should be shifted to the environment in which people apply their skills. An environment conducive to mobilizing social groups and motivating individuals are basic requirements for promoting capacity utilization and retention' (Hopkins, 1994: 4[iii]).

From a Local First perspective, current approaches to capacity assessment have three limitations:

- **A needs assessment is made without an accompanying capacity assessment.**
  If a needs assessment is conducted without a parallel capacity assessment that looks at which local institutions at local, state and national level are currently meeting the identified needs and how they are doing so, or could do so with additional resources, then almost inevitably external delivery solutions will be sought.

- **There is insufficient attention given to the methodology for seeking out capacity in non-traditional places (the assumption is that the players in any particular sphere are easy to identify).**
  In any sector, it is easy to identify the central government agencies that have responsibility for delivering services. Strengthening their capacity, if done effectively, is clearly a very high priority. But the capacity to deliver may also be found in far-flung places, beyond the capital city, through particularly effective state and local government institutions, through civil society networks[11] or organisations, or in the private sector. Justice is a prime example where in many low income countries, particularly post-conflict and fragile states, a vanishingly small proportion of justice is provided by the formal state sector.[12]

---

11 *For descriptions of civil society networks in many environmental fields operating at a large scale, see: How to Make Poverty History: the Central Role of Local Organisations in Meeting the MDGs. Tom Bigg and David Satterthwaite (eds.). London: International Institute for Environment and Development (IIED), 2005; http://pubs.iied.org/pdfs/11000IIED.pdf.*

12 *In Sierra Leone, only 15 per cent of justice is delivered by the central justice sector, with approximately 85 per cent of the population falling under the jurisdiction of customary law, defined by the constitution as 'the rules of law, which, by custom, are applicable to particular communities in Sierra Leone'. Source: Leila Chirayath, Caroline Sage and Michael Woolcock, 'Customary Law and Policy Reform: Engaging with the Plurality of Justice Systems', World Bank background paper (2005: 3); http://siteresources.worldbank.org/INTWDR2006/Resources/477383-1118673432908/Customary_Law_and_Policy_Reform.pdf. Likewise in Malawi, between 80 and 90 per cent of all disputes are processed through traditional justice forums. Source:Wilfried Scharf, 'Non-State Justice Systems in Sothern Africa: How Should Governments Respond?', Cape Town: University of Cape Town, no date. In Bangladesh, an estimated 60 to 70 per cent of all disputes are processed*

An effective capacity assessment would need to review the functioning of traditional justice systems and new innovations such as land courts, as well as mechanisms to hold the formal justice systems to account, and develop a strategy that built on strengths that already exist and takes account of the role of non-governmental organisations in challenging and improving the formal sector.

• **The approach is a deficit model, whereby individuals and organisations are assessed against a predetermined set of criteria, with the aim of identifying where their capacity should be improved rather than looking to see what contribution organisations are already capable of making and supporting that contribution.**
The capacity that Local First prioritises is the capacity for innovation and entrepreneurship – for seeing opportunities and devising effective ways to exploit them, for taking existing local practices and adapting and improving them, and above all, for listening to the demands and needs of the population and seeking to meet them. Theoretical models can be useful in framing assessments, but they need to be models that focus on what an organisation has already achieved and what it could achieve in the future with resources and appropriate partnerships, not whether it meets or fails to meet certain technical criteria. Against these, local organisations will always look weak compared to the multilateral organisations which frame such models.

How could a capacity assessment look from a Local First perspective?

Suppose a funder wishes to find local organisations to lead a long-term programme to provide a safety net for AIDS orphans. Like any other talent search, this can be broken down into three stages:
• Establishing who is out there.
• Assessing their capacity.
• Identifying how best to use that capacity.

---

through customary law. See: Programming for Justice: Access for All. A Practitioner's Guide to a Human Rights-Based Approach to Access to Justice. Bangkok: UNDP, 2005; http://www.apjrf.com/APJRF%20Content/UNDP%20-%20Programming%20For%20 Justice%20-%20Access%20For%20All.pdf.

The capacity assessment or talent search can be contracted out to an international or a local consultancy, but crucially, with a goal of finding an organisation, coalition or network that can lead the programme from within the country, with whatever partnership support may be necessary.

- **Establishing who is out there and what they are doing**
  There is a range of ways this can be done, for example using databases, networks, or competitions. It will be important to ensure that organisations based beyond the capital city have an equal chance to be included, and that those assessing capacity travel widely to meet and assess potential partners. Increasingly, social media will provide effective ways to put the word out for expressions of interest, and the search for talent may look very different in five years' time. However, all of these approaches will come up against limits and there is no substitute for getting out into the field to find local partners.
  Rarely is it the case that no one will be found to be active, although they may not conform to Western notions of a formal organisation. Were that the case, it could be interpreted as a warning sign about the importance of the issue locally.
  The value of this broad approach is that it also provides a way of quantifying what is already being done, identifying areas of strength and those where little service is being provided. This will be essential in shaping the new initiative.

- **Assessing their capacity**
  Key to Local First is to find organisations with both a track record of work to date – this may be quite small-scale – and a strategic view of how the work could have greater impact and scale. It is also essential to exclude the vast array of briefcase NGOs – those with little genuine activity which have been created by insufficiently critical use of donor funds. (See Bano, 2012: 135, table 5.5, which demonstrates a stark distinction in the Pakistani context between voluntary organisations and NGOs. In Pakistan at least, they appear as two completely distinct species of organisation.) A request for written documents will test the organisation's track record, vision, understanding of the drivers of violence, knowledge of who

else is working in the field, and how they might collaborate with others. It will also be essential to talk in depth to people who know the organisation and its work.

Local First places a great emphasis on the engagement of voluntary effort. This is partly because development challenges are so huge that they are unlikely to be met entirely through paid staff. But it is also because the ability to harness volunteer effort may be an important proxy for effectiveness and legitimacy. By contrast, asking target beneficiaries about the reputation of a provider of public goods may not yield honest answers, especially in a context where it may seem as though funding will be granted or withdrawn. Beneficiaries may well decide to play safe and give a positive picture in order to secure continuing resources.

- **Identifying how best to use that capacity**
  One of the key themes of these case studies is the need for partnership. It is unlikely that any organisation on its own will be effective, so the mandate for the chosen organisation or organisations must include a specification of how they will link up with other relevant organisations.

Suggestion 2: Make a commitment to using external organisations as a last resort, not a first resort, and as supportive partners to local organisations, not as contractors.

There is considerable inertia in the system and an understandable desire on the part of organisations charged with using public money wisely to continue with tried and tested methods, including those that prioritise the use of external agencies. Hence even with the determination of the head of USAID to increase the proportion of its resources going directly to local organisations and governments to 30 per cent, the proportion going to US commercial contractors actually went up in 2011.[13]

For some donors, there are also issues of scale and of capacity to absorb funds, which make it difficult to transition to making greater direct use of local organisations. This is where networks, including trade associations and other professional associations, can be a vital

---

13 Source: *www.foreignpolicy.com/articles/2012/07/18/hired_gun_fight.*

link in the chain, enabling large-scale initiatives without losing local ownership and volunteerism.

One of the defining features of the case studies is the quality and variety of the partnerships they embody between local and external organisations, as well as between different local institutions. A genuine and effective partnership from an external organisation will:

- Support the local partner's strategy, not seek to impose an internationally proven one.
- Make full use of the local knowledge and legitimacy of the local partner.
- Provide support in terms of organisational development, but in a framework of mutual learning.
- Adapt its role to the partner's changing capacity, aiming to end dependence over time and nurture self-reliance.

Suggestion 3: Identify a few sectors within which to experiment with a Local First approach and aim over time to target an increasing percentage of funding within those sectors to locally led or locally owned programmes.

Measurable targets are important in forcing change, so it is not surprising that these are increasingly being mentioned as a way of shifting the emphasis towards a Local First approach. As well as the USAID target mentioned above, the UK International Development Committee recently recommended that 10 per cent of UK aid to DRC should go to local organisations.[14]

This approach can be applied equally to procurement of goods and services from the commercial sector, and to use of NGOs to provide services in sensitive areas such as justice, security and accountability – all areas where trust is critically important and where a stronger civil society presence is also likely to improve government performance, as the case studies show. The Building Markets case study indicates that shifting to local procurement enabled funds from DfID and CIDA to create an additional 130,000 part-time jobs in Afghanistan. While the particular circumstances of Afghanistan meant that many of these were not permanent, in other countries it may be possible to put more focus on procurement of goods and services with a broader local market.

---

14 *International Development Select Committee report. Working Effectively in Fragile and Conflict-Affected States: DRC and Rwanda. London, 2012.*

In order for this approach to succeed, funders will somehow need to bridge the gap between their staff and the universe of effective local organisations. Some donors have done this by placing staff in the field on a long-term basis so that they can monitor which organisations, in whatever sector, are really capable of delivering. USAID was praised for its commitment of staff in South Sudan, which evaluators felt had made the work they funded more consistently successful than that of other donors.[15]

Suggestion 4: Commit to long-term evaluations of impact, sustainability and value for money from locally led versus internationally led projects.

The difficulty of comparing value for money and impact in projects where local and international efforts are closely intertwined already has been mentioned. If they are going to scale up, locally led programmes will almost always need external funding. Some sort of support generally accompanies such funding. Nevertheless, if Local First is an idea worth testing, then evaluations need to be able to distinguish between programmes with local leadership and programmes where leadership comes from outside.

Success or failure needs to be viewed over at least a five-year time frame and needs to capture impact that goes beyond what was specified at the outset (eg, in the log frame) in order to assess the added value of having locals working as principals, not just as agents. At the end of the evaluation period, there needs to be a judgement as to how sustainable the programme is going forward and what its legacy has been or will be if funding ceases.

Suggestion 5: Enable structures that allow local organisations to scale up their impact.

A serious commitment to Local First will recognise that consistent funding is needed if local organisations are to be able to match the scale that multilaterals and INGOs can operate at. As they scale up, local organisations will need funding and possibly support with core functions such as finance, governance and measurement of impact.

---

15 *Source: J. Bennett, S. Pantuliano, W. Fenton, A. Vaux, C. Barnett, E. Brusset. Aiding the Peace: A Multi-Donor Evaluation of Support to Conflict Prevention and Peacebuilding Activities in Southern Sudan 2005-2010. ITAD Ltd: UK, 2010.*

This support may be to organisations, networks or, like the organisations that feature in these case studies, to organisations with extensive networks of paid and volunteer staff in different parts of a country. One of the key features of successful models is the coming together of a number of donors to fund a particular institution, as has happened with the International HIV/AIDS Alliance, which channels funding from a number of donors to 1,700 community-based organisations in 40 countries and with PeaceNet, a Kenyan network of peace organisations.

Donors who grasp the point that strong local organisations are a key element in stimulating better government performance need to fund them in an equally consistent way. This will also make it easier to reach whatever target they set for funds to go directly to local organisations, as they will be building capable, accountable and responsive organisations that are able to scale up. (See Box F.)

Suggestion 6: Ensure that all evaluations include an assessment of the impact of the project on the growth or decline in local capacity.

In the UK government's recent, extremely thorough, review of multilateral organisations, the organisations were judged against 41 criteria.[16] However, none of the criteria referred to the organisations' success in transferring responsibility to local organisations. This could be construed as an assumption that the need for multilaterals' presence will never end.

If the ultimate goal of aid is for countries to graduate from receiving it in order to be self-reliant, it surely makes more sense to have explicit goals in every programme about the extent to which, at the end of the programme, local organisations, whether public sector, private sector or non-profit, have taken over aspects of delivery.

Such an approach would recognise the contribution of multilaterals, or indeed INGOs, but would view this as explicitly transitional, and would seek to accelerate the transition.

Suggestions for INGOs

Suggestion 7: Evaluate in what ways organisational practice is locally led or locally owned, and how this can be demonstrated.

---

16 Source: *DfID Multilateral Aid Review, 2011.*

Box F

The Danish development agency, DANIDA, has an interesting funding approach in which it identifies key local NGOs doing good work and provides them with relatively long-term core funding. Given the complex challenges of peacebuilding, it is generally agreed that long-term funding commitments are necessary. This was, for example, the case with their support for the Nepali organisation, Alliance for Peace, a local NGO founded by Dipendra Tamang.

Source: Peace Nexus, Peace Direct Local Engagement Project, 2011.

INGOs working in different fields will have different starting points. Locally led may be much easier in the field of development, where timescales are relatively long, than in humanitarian work, where a rapid initial response is needed. Locally led may be essential in fields where trust is paramount, such as peacebuilding, and perceived as less important in more technical fields.

Nevertheless, anyone working in development must surely see their ultimate goal as to have empowered people to do their own development and become self-reliant. Therefore, a logical first step is for organisations to reflect on how their ways of working get them closer to this goal, formulate a claim and determine how this claim would be measured.

For example, a claim that local partners set the strategic direction of their work, with the INGO finding the resources that are needed to put this into practice, could be measured through an independent survey of partners. A claim about local procurement could be validated by an audit of procurement practices.

Suggestion 8: Set a goal to increase the Local First orientation of their work, and define how this increase can be demonstrated.

A second step is to look for areas of improvement and set goals. For example, this could be a goal to directly channel a greater percentage of funds to local organisations, rather than through the organisation's local staff, or to ensure that all evaluations measure the extent to which responsibility and capacity has been transferred to the local partner. These goals will need clear measurement targets.

Suggestion 9: Make a practice of seeking out local suppliers of goods and services, including audit, market research and evaluation.

A concerted move by INGOs to use services such as audit, market research and evaluation from local suppliers would help to create employment locally, as well as having other benefits – local evaluation staff can travel to areas out of bounds to international staff, and local auditors may have a better appreciation of country specific issues. Where local organisations of the required competence cannot be found, it would be good practice for donors to allocate funds for training that could bring them up to the required standard over time, as Building Markets has done with a range of suppliers of goods and services.

Suggestions for local NGOs

Suggestion 10: Seek funding and support on the organisation's own terms insofar as possible and resist being cast as delivery agents.

Local organisations face difficult choices when they are asked by funders to deliver programmes that they believe to be sub-optimal, or even likely to fail. Taking on the contract ensures the organisation survives and may enable it to keep its own programmes going, but risks tarnishing the organisation's reputation as one that responds to genuine community needs.

Local organisations should at least remain clear about why they are undertaking a particular piece of work and resist losing sight of their ability to set their own priorities.

Suggestion 11: Maintain the involvement of the wider community as volunteers and ensure that the organisation has a survival strategy in the absence of external funding.

Local organisations that want to scale up their impact need to consciously safeguard their ability to continue to operate in the absence of funding from international sources. Funders can be fickle, more often facing constraints of their own that work against long-term funding relationships, while host governments may impose restrictions on funding from outside the country. Hence local organisations need to cultivate local sources of funding and have in mind a strategy to protect the capacity they have put in place, where possible through generating local funds.

Suggestion 12: Remunerate paid staff in keeping with local wage rates.

Local organisations that look to the long-term need to safeguard their ability to mobilise volunteer effort and to have a wage structure that is sustainable. Both require salaries to retain a relationship with local wages, which may be a particular challenge where an influx of aid has led to widespread distortion of the market for goods and services, as well as salaries. The authors of these case studies have seen their partners on a number of occasions go without any salary in order to preserve the organisation. This is not desirable, but it is a strong indication of their motivation.

Suggestion 13: Seek to connect community-based activity with local and national government, as well as with the work of INGOs and multilaterals, in order to coordinate with and influence them.

Local organisations need to play their part in achieving a degree of coordination between their work and the initiatives of multilaterals, and local and national governments. They have valuable insights to contribute, and their work will be easier and more effective if these insights inform the work of other actors. This is a long-term endeavour, but important both in its own right and because it will be an important touchstone for donors seeking a joined-up approach.

References

Alusala, Nelson. Reintegrating Ex-combatants in the Great Lakes Region: Lessons Learned. Monograph 179. Pretoria: Institute for Security Studies, 2011.
Bano, Masooda. Breakdown in Pakistan: How Aid is Eroding Institutions for Collective Action. Stanford: Stanford University Press, 2012.
Booth, David. Towards a Theory of Local Governance and Public Goods

Provision in Sub-Saharan Africa. London: Overseas Development Institute. Africa Power and Politics Programme (APPP), Working Paper 13, 2010.

Chopra, Tanja, Christian Ranheim and Rod Nixon. *'Local-Level Justice Under Transitional Administration: Lessons from East Timor', in From Customary Justice and the Rule of Law in War-Torn Societies. Deborah Isser, Ed. Washington, DC: USIP Press Books, 2011.*

Gillhespy, Tom and Carolyn Hayman. *Coming Home: A case study of community led Disarmament, Demobilization and Reintegration in DR Congo. London: Peace Direct, 2011.*

Hopkins, Thomas J. *Handbook on Capacity Assessment Methodologies – an Analytical Review. New York: UNDP, 1994.*

Joshi, Anuradha and Peter Houtzager. *'Widgets or Watchdogs? Conceptual Explorations in Social Accountability', Public Management Review Volume 14, Issue 2, February 2012.*

Kelsall, Tim. *Going With the Grain in African Development? London: Overseas Development Institute. Africa Power and Politics Programme (APPP), Working Paper 1, 2008.*

Shivakumar, Sujai. *The Constitution of Development: Crafting Capabilities for Self-Governance. New York: Palgrave Macmillan, 2005.*

US Senate Committee on Foreign Relations. *Evaluating US Foreign Assistance to Afghanistan. Washington: US Senate, 2011.*

. . . .

Connecting disarmament, demobilisation and reintegration realities in DR Congo: CRC

by Hans Rouw

This volume begins with a case study demonstrating the relevance of Local First in the context of active conflict in eastern DRC. As this portrait of the Centre Résolution Conflits (CRC) demonstrates, trust and long-term commitment are essential ingredients for supporting the reintegration of ex-combatants into their communities. Two key aspects of Local First are evident here: sustainability and voluntarism. Locally led organisations like CRC play an indispensable role in sustaining the results of international interventions precisely because they are able to engage ex-combatants and their communities within the context of their daily lives. The effectiveness of the CRC approach is verified in the large amount of voluntary time that its members donate in the course of a year – over 4,000 hours per task force. Indicators to measure the impact of CRC's work that are devised by local communities themselves can also contribute to a deeper understanding about how to implement DDR processes with greater success.

'Congo is a discourse. In reality it does not exist' – Former combatant in Butembo, North Kivu (Rouw and Willems, 2010: 5).

Brief conflict analysis

Parts of eastern Democratic Republic of Congo (DRC), known as the Kivus, have been plagued by complex cycles of conflict for decades. During the 1990s, discrepancies between traditional and state law related to land ownership in Kivu enabled a few to grab resource-rich land at the cost of many. This also escalated existing ethnic tensions, which were exacerbated by an influx of refugees and Interhamwe[1] from Rwanda after the 1994 genocide. The

---

1 *The Hutu Interahamwe which fled into DRC would later form the basis of the Forces Démocratiques de Libération du Rwanda (FDLR).*

Map showing impact of project

weakening of Mobutu's rule over Zaire in the 1990s encouraged Zaire's neighbours to support the rebellion led by Kabila and his Alliance des Forces Démocratiques pour la Liberation du Congo (AFDL) in an attempt to access Zaire's mineral wealth. Kabila's AFDL, joined by Tutsi militias, marched from the east to Kinshasa and ousted President Mobutu from power in May 1997, renaming the country the Democratic Republic of the Congo.

Once in power, Kabila attempted to curb the influence of his former allies, demanding that Rwandan and Ugandan troops leave the country. In response, Uganda and Rwanda supported the formation of a new rebel movement, the Rassemblement Congolais pour la Démocratie (RCD), which occupied eastern DRC and ignited Congo's Second War in August 1998. Zimbabwe, Angola and Namibia supported Kabila, whilst Rwanda and Uganda backed various opposing rebel groups. In July 2002, a peace agreement was signed stipulating the withdrawal of the Rwandan Army, and the dismantling of ex-FAR (Forces Armées Rwandaise) and Interahamwe. In September that same year, a similar agreement was signed with Uganda. All previous agreements were combined into one document, referred to as the 'Final Act', which was signed in Sun City, South Africa in April 2003. The estimated death toll related to violent conflict in eastern DRC since 1998 ranges from 2.5 million to 5.4 million,[2] with hundreds of thousands[3] of people being internally displaced as a consequence of war.

Despite the peace agreement, violence in the Kivus continued, most notably by the Forces démocratiques de libération du Rwanda (FDLR), Congrès National pour la Défense de la Peuple (CNDP) and various Mai Mai groups.[4] At present, Kivu still remains insecure. For instance, in May and June 2012, the Congolese army was involved in fierce stop-start fighting in North Kivu province, with renegade soldiers loyal to former rebel commander Bosco Ntaganda forcing about 100,000 civilians to flee for their lives.[5] More generally, eastern DRC suffers from weak governance and security actors who are largely incapable and/or unmotivated to protect the civilian population. The renewed UN mission, MONUSCO, aims to assist the government of DRC with a Protection of Civilians mandate, but is unable to consistently provide protection throughout the vast geographical area of eastern DRC.[6]

In North Kivu, many of the estimated population of about 5 million[7] people suffer on a daily basis and consequently have lost trust in the capacity of their government to resolve the issues facing this part of DRC. These issues include violent ways of accessing eastern DRC's abundant resources, myriad armed groups, the reintegration of militia groups into the national army, ethnic conflicts, underdevelopment, ongoing land disputes and large numbers of Internally Displaced Persons (IDPs) and refugees.

---

2 For discussion, see: http://www.hsrgroup.org/docs/Publications/HSR2009/2009Human Security Report_Pt2_3_DeathTollDemocraticRepublic.pdf.

3 See: http://www.internal-displacement.org/idmc/website/countries.nsf/%28httpEnvelo pes%29/96849E3579EE3240C12577FC0044524A?OpenDocument.

4 'Mai Mai' is a collective term for self-defence militias claiming to fight for the safety and security of their local communities, as well as against foreign oppression.

5 Bosco Ntaganda, also known as the 'Terminator', is the military commander of the Congrès national pour la défense du peuple (CNDP) and is wanted by the International Criminal Court in The Hague for alleged war crimes.

6 The current UN mission, MONUSCO, was preceded by MONUC, which was put in place in 2000, after 50,000 people had been killed and 500,000 people had been displaced in Ituri (situated north of the Kivus in Province Orientale). Whilst MONUC established bases in Haut and Bas Uele districts, it could do little about the many other local conflicts raging in the area. For more information on MONUSCO, see: http://monusco.unmissions.org/.

7 See: http://www.provincenordkivu.org/presentation.html.

Conflict transformation: the missing links

'Not knowing the problem is the problem' (Rouw and Willems, 2010: 25).

Two key challenges to address in fragile states like DRC are the lack of social cohesion, and the need to restore confidence and links between civilians and their government. Much more than it damages buildings and physical infrastructures, conflict destroys trust and relationships, as well as the capacity and will of people to work together. These intangible qualities must be rebuilt if peace is to be sustainable. The necessary work, then, is done most effectively when language, culture, and understanding of the effects of conflict are acknowledged and shared. In other words, it is vital to know the problem to be able to actually address it constructively. Restoring confidence between civilians and governance actors is needed to create forms of cooperation designed to address issues of conflict together. However, in the words of CRC's current coordinator, 'The members of government are another country' (Rouw and Willems, 2009: unpublished field notes).

When they first began their work in 1993 in Bunia, Ituri, the founders of the Centre Résolution Conflits (CRC) realised that local insight and trust are key issues. Formally registered as a Congolese non-governmental organisation (NGO) in 1997, CRC expanded its work to Nyakunde and Beni from 2004 onward. Initial CRC activities had a general focus on teaching conflict transformation skills to communities, after which attention became specifically focussed on youth populations because they are the leaders of tomorrow. Since then, CRC has expanded to include media sensitisation, local negotiations with militia leaders and support to displaced people.

CRC now works on all these issues throughout North Kivu and Ituri with a 17 member full-time staff, a network of part-time staff and large groups of volunteers who participate in local task forces. A strong religious faith provides the facilitative framework within which the organisation operates. Through the course of its work, CRC staff has experienced the horrors of the raging conflicts in Kivu first-hand: when the organisation's deputy director and his family were murdered in 2002, and again in 2004, when their office in Bunia was ransacked by militia forces.

Since its inception, CRC has been dedicated to creating conflict transformation activities that are contextually appropriate and aim to mitigate the violent components of conflict in eastern DRC. The organisation has always concentrated on uncovering the problems of local communities and worked towards local solutions. 'The main thing is to start with grassroots people,' says CRC co-founder, Kongosi Onia Mussanzi, who goes on to explain that, 'when we used to talk with people, we used to give the example of a river, and if the river is polluted, you can't start if it is polluted from the source. You can't say now we are here, let us start working here. You have to go to the source, and from there, you go slowly down the river. And thus peace means starting with the grassroots, dealing with the people who are living the impact of the conflict' (Cairns, 2011: 5). CRC believes that befriending enemies and teaching people how to resolve conflict in peaceful ways is the only sustainable approach to ending war and rebuilding community life. In short, people are part of the problem and therefore must be part of the solution.

As militia groups are the primary source of violence in the conflicts in eastern DRC, international responses to the challenges of militia violence have focused on disarmament, demobilisation and reintegration (DDR) programmes. A myriad of rebel groups have operated in North Kivu in the last decade. For example, there is the Rwandese Forces démocratiques de libération du Rwanda (FDLR) and the Congrès national pour la défense du peuple (CNDP); there also have been Uganda's Allied Democratic Forces (ADF) and Mai Mai militias, such as the Patriotes Resistants Congolais (Pareco). The Mai Mai were established in the absence of any other source of protection as a reaction to the foreign or proxy forces operating in eastern DRC. Over time, some of these groups turned war into a profitable business by controlling mines and joining in banditry.

The DDR programme in the Kivus can be divided into three strands: the Commission Nationale du Désarmament, de la Démobilisation et de la Réinsertion (CONADER); the international Disarmament, Demobilization, Repatriation, Resettlement and Reintegration (DDRRR) programme; and the programme for demobilising child soldiers. In 2008, after the signing of the Goma Agreement between 22 militia groups and the DRC government, the Amani[8] DDR programme also started in the Kivus.

---

8 *The Amani programme was part of the national programme (ie CONADER), but*

DDR programmes often have a difficult time connecting with local realities in ways that create sustainable solutions to the threat of armed groups, especially in terms of reintegration issues. However, it is vital to understand 'the "laws of the bush" ... in order to break the cycle of returning to the militia. Reintegration must connect to life experienced by the combatants' (Rouw and Willems, 2010: 35). As an evaluation of the Multi-country Demobilization and Reintegration Programme[9] (MDRP) notes:

'Experience shows that the design of reintegration programmes should, as a matter of priority, include a clear understanding of the social, cultural, economic and political dynamics of both ex-combatants and the recipient communities. An understanding of these aspects should inform the planning of a reintegration programme and hence its sustainability. More often, however, DDR programmes have been designed with little or no consideration for either ex-combatants or the communities they are to be reintegrated into' *(Alusala, 2011: iv).*

In contrast, CRC operates community-based programmes that work both with ex-combatants and their recipient communities, supporting former combatants in being accepted by their communities, as well as providing a source of livelihood for these people and their families. In particular, as indicated in an interview with 12 NGOs at a meeting on 12 November 2009 in Butembo, CRC works within an integrated community-based model that taps deep into a community's voluntary capacity for rebuilding itself because 'international strategies were "interventions", whereas solutions should be more home grown and aim for a longer term. There should be more connections between the demobilised and the communities of integration' (Rouw and Willems, 2009: unpublished field notes).

Through this approach, CRC has become a key link between communities, local government authorities in eastern DRC and

---

it was designed specifically for the Kivus.
9 *The MDRP was a multi-donor programme that operated between 2002 and 2009 in the Great Lakes Region and claims to have demobilised close to 300,000 combatants and supported 232,000 former combatants in their reintegration. For more detailed information, see: http://www.mdrp.org.*

militia groups in the bush, facilitating numerous negotiations for the return of armed militia members and child soldiers.

The CRC approach

CRC has developed a clear theory of change: by reducing the number of active combatants and sustainably reintegrating them, the level of violence in communities will be reduced, allowing for the broader community development necessary for lasting peace. Rather than DDR, CRC uses an RDD approach – reintegration, disarmament and demobilisation – because it is the effectiveness of the community reintegration process that influences militia members who want to disarm, as well as secures their long-term demobilisation. CRC assisted the disarmament and demobilisation of 4,276 combatants (3,532 men; 270 women; 474 children), of whom 1,334 were reintegrated into cooperatives; 1,078 into the police; 1,120 into the army and 774 given other kinds of reintegration assistance (Gillhespy and Hayman, 2011: 14).

Based on past experience, CRC's current work primarily focuses on an established process of engaging with militia groups. First and foremost, this means building credibility and trust with these armed groups. Sensitisation then needs to take place with both the militias and the recipient communities. Sensitisation here means 'knowing all sides of the conflict and being able to understand all sides. The emphasis should be on what people want out of their life' (Rouw and Willems, 2010: 34). Negotiating the surrender of militia groups then follows after sensitisation has taken place.

In January 2008, CRC began contacting armed groups in order to address increasing levels of violence in select communities in North Kivu. Initial contact always takes place through a *port de parole*, or someone who is familiar to the group and trusted, such as family members or friends of key militia leaders or members. Once contact has been established, a CRC staff person speaks with the key person on the phone in order to arrange a first meeting, which takes place in a neutral venue. On average, three or four meetings are necessary to gain trust and build credibility. However, the timeframe for these meetings differs in each case, depending on the complexity of the problems to be resolved.

The next step involves meetings between CRC and the broader membership of the militia group in order to talk about the goals of the group, their motivation for continuing to remain in the group, their outlook on life, and so on. Importantly, contact with key individuals and other militia members must be continually maintained, as such groups tend to split up, change their membership or leadership, or change alliances between militia groups. Ongoing engagement is also the way to stop the cycle of re-recruitment by militias. As such, the CRC approach demands a lot of energy and resources, which is the case even before it becomes clear whether demobilisation and reintegration efforts will be successful.

Creating momentum for peace is closely linked to CRC's overall approach, especially in terms of the organisation's emphasis on RDD rather than DDR. That is, efforts to persuade militia members to leave the bush begin with talking through the possibilities and benefits of actual reintegration into the communities. This is deemed necessary to motivate militia members and show that returning home will provide them with other opportunities than are available to them in the bush.

Significantly, this part of CRC's process also addresses the fact that former combatants often stay in contact with their former colleagues who chose to remain with the militia group. This allows CRC to tap into the potential of former combatants as interlocutors for demobilisation and peace.

Through CRC's engagement with (former) combatants before, during and after their RDD work, only 10 per cent of former combatants indicated that they were considering a return to the bush, whereas 58 per cent of former combatants who did not engage with the CRC process indicated that they were considering a return (Gillhespy and Hayman, 2011: 21). CRC's RDD process adds value to the international DDR programmes in the Kivus precisely because they can engage (former) combatants and their communities within the context of their daily lives. Despite the fact that these former combatants all participated in a DDR programme, it becomes clear that facilitating the DDR process, as CRC approaches this, increases the chances of the DDR programme having more sustainable results.

In addition to the sensitisation stage (ie, persuading combatants to leave their militia groups and persuading their communities to accept them back), the CRC approach to reintegration includes four other key elements:

- Provision of a range of livelihood options, some of which are also open to members of the community.
- Reparation programmes are sometimes included in the re-integration process, whereby former militia members build roads or other facilities to benefit the community.
- Building social networks based largely on voluntary effort, which sustains the RDD process at the micro level over time.
- Context-specific indicators that measure success over the long term, not just at the point where a combatant leaves the militia group and disarms.

In general, the period between being a combatant and becoming a respected community member is long and arduous. For example, according to a former combatant in Mwenga, North Kivu, social acceptance by the community may take up to more than five years in some cases (Rouw and Willems, 2010: 35). Combatants attempting to reintegrate into their local communities generally remain in limbo between civilian life and the bush for some time, in large part depending on their personal experiences and the time they spent as combatants.

This is exemplified by Lea.[10] In a group discussion on reintegrating into civilian life, she showed the identity card she had obtained after she demobilised, whilst at the same time revealing the combat fatigues she was wearing under her traditional dress. In effect, this combination of civilian and militia life enables her to go either way, depending on how circumstances evolve for her (*ibid*, 25). Lea's position between both options suggests that the practical and social support that CRC provides is greatly needed.

Organisational structures in CRC's work

CRC is a small organisation that aims to increase its scope and en-hance the sustainability of its work. Therefore, CRC staff decided to branch out through initiatives such as task forces, radio shows and cooperatives. Such initiatives serve to multiply, deepen and extend the reach of CRC work.

---

10 *For reasons of security this is not her real name.*

Establishing task forces

Since 2004, through its community conflict resolution training programmes, CRC has encouraged each community to create a local peace committee. The ongoing relationships that have been built by participation in the local peace committees have created a framework through which CRC has been able to introduce the livelihood support component of its RDD process. CRC regularly follows up with these committees to monitor how they are working. In cases where a local peace committee is no longer active, CRC instead works with a local development organisation.

With additional funding from the Baring Foundation, since 2009 CRC has been able to build on some of its local peace committees to establish six task forces in Beni, Butembo, Bunia, Aveba, Mambasa and Kasenyi-Tchomia. Each task force has an average of 12 members, who range from community and religious leaders to former child soldiers and even former militia commanders. The goal of these task forces is to bring together key community leaders who have been involved in addressing local conflicts, whilst ensuring that all sectors of the community are represented. Task force membership has remained consistent since they were first established, apart from the deaths of two members, one from natural causes and one who was killed whilst undertaking work for the task force. Task force members are trained by a three-person team from CRC that includes the heads of the human rights and ex-combatants programmes, as well as CRC director, Henri Bura Ladyi. These training sessions have a twofold purpose: to explain how a task force should report to CRC: and how to effectively evaluate their own work.

The Butembo Task Force has met on a weekly basis since 24 July 2009. Most other task forces meet together once a month. All of the task forces meet with CRC staff at regular intervals throughout the year (usually on a quarterly basis) and submit regular reports on their activities to CRC. Whilst the task forces primarily were created to assist in negotiating with militia groups, they have now taken on a wider role, acting as an early warning system for CRC and local level conflict resolution. As such, they have evolved into groups with an important role to play in supporting the recovery of their communities as they emerge from violent conflict: they help reduce violence and thus make development possible.

Radio broadcasts

In an area where communication and transportation services are very limited, radio is an important means of communication for CRC. Since 2009, CRC has been using radio intensively and effectively to encourage combatants to leave their armed groups. Between 2009 and 2011, 156 programmes have been broadcast through three local radio stations: Radio Moto in Butembo; RTEB in Beni; and Radio Candip in Bunia. In particular, short slogans with strong, clear messages are regularly broadcast: 'We can't build our country living in the bush. We can't build our country through violence. We can't build our country through raping women' (Cairns, 2011: 16).

The power of using radio as a means to sensitise combatants is perhaps best demonstrated by the fact that many who return to their villages immediately join the local radio club. In doing so, they create an effective link between the community and other combatants who are still active. Whilst those who have left no longer see their former colleagues, 'Through the radio they can immediately address them with precision to show what they have found in the village and that they would do better to follow them' (*ibid*, 20). This kind of personal sensitisation makes it easier to demobilise large numbers of young militia members quickly. As one ex-combatant explains, 'I can say I am Kidicho, I have been there with you, now I am here, you hear my voice, come to join me here. They even cite the name. You, I know you are there, I know you have been shot by the bullet. I know your wife. I know you are living on that mountain. I am already good here, you can come and join me' (*ibid*). Radio is, therefore, a direct way for ex-combatants to encourage their former colleagues to also return to their own communities.

Joint civilian and ex-combatant cooperatives

Another key component to CRC's success has been the establishment of cooperatives that enable civilians and former combatants to work together on joint projects. Former combatants are provided with livelihood support and civilians are included to prevent frustration and alienation. Perceptions of rewarding the perpetrator can emerge when only former combatants are given livelihood support and victims are left to their own devices. Moreover, these joint projects can help reduce prejudice on both sides whilst surrounding former combatants with social guidance and affirmation of acceptable moral behaviour. In some cases, ex-combatant membership in a cooperative is linked to making reparations to their local communities by rehabilitating local infrastructures.

With a current total of 24 cooperatives established since 2009, members are selected by the communities themselves. Initially, a cooperative has 30 members and receives US$2,000 in financial support from CRC. It is then up to cooperative members to decide if they wish to include new members (all of which have done so). In some cases, this has resulted in cooperatives of up to 200 members. On the one hand, this is a strong indicator of the success of this approach. But on the other, this poses challenges related to the organisation and financing of the cooperatives. Currently, CRC addresses this by restricting the number of core cooperative members, whilst enabling broader membership through microfinance schemes.

A community-based approach

CRC brings a deep, long-term commitment to the communities in which it works, which is facilitated by the task forces. This commitment is what convinces communities to support and contribute to CRC activities. Built up over years of engagement, CRC's credibility with communities has proven to be a crucial ingredient for making its work possible and successful. In adopting a thoroughly community-based approach, CRC aims to facilitate and empower former combatants and local communities to engage in self-help processes related to local development, as well as to enhance their own security. In general, CRC's community-based approach seeks to involve a fully representative selection of local community interests and concerns, which is reflected in all of its activities.

More specifically, CRC's approach to its community-based RDD process recognises that engaging with armed groups for peace is only possible by connecting with the reasons an armed group exists. The CRC approach is also based on the necessity of understanding communities in their own context and engaging them through social networks for peace. This can only happen constructively and sustainably when CRC's work and networks connect with the day-to-day challenges of communities and former combatants alike. Perhaps the best evidence that CRC is largely successful in tapping into the day-to-day challenges faced by the communities in which they work is the fact that task force members put in large amounts of voluntary time, at least 4,432 hours per task force per year.[11]

For example, whilst CRC's livelihood activities primarily focus on former combatants and women, other community residents also have become involved because they see how these projects benefit their communities. At the same time, CRC's radio club programmes have tapped into a deep community desire for peace and development, as well as provide a structure for constructive self-help rebuilding.

Connecting insiders and outsiders for peacebuilding

Reintegration and peacebuilding are complex and dynamic processes that require several different roles and responsibilities. Some of these are best played by insiders like CRC and their task forces, whereas others are better suited for outside actors, such as MONUSCO. Ideally, top-down and bottom-up components of DDR (or indeed RDD) should complement one another and add value. On the one hand, for example, CRC is able to bridge the gap between the concept of DDR and the actual practise in the field. The organisation is also able to link (former) combatants and their communities for sustained social and livelihood support in reintegration. On the other hand, the international community that supports DDR in eastern DRC is able to manage DDR facilities, register former combatants and give them identification cards, offer transport to DDR facilities and provide services, such as reintegration kits, training and sometimes development schemes. In short, information, working modalities, facilities and resources need to be shared between insiders and outsiders to attain the optimum mix of actions towards engagement for peacebuilding.

A practical example of effective insider-outsider cooperation was explained by CRC's coordinator, Henri, during meetings at The Hague.[12] After prolonged negotiation between CRC and a Mai

---

11 *This estimate of time is calculated on the basis of each member contributing two hours of their time per month (or in Butembo, per week) to attend task force meetings. However, members each contribute time between meetings to investigate problems, incidents and rumours reported to them. Thus the voluntary time spent by them likely is much greater than the estimate given (Cairns, 2011: 15).*

12 *This meeting was organised by the Dutch Peace, Security and Development Network on 1 December 2011 in The Hague. See: http://www.psdnetwork.nl/.*

Mai group, their commander decided to go to a DDR camp run by MONUSCO. Pride and the potential loss of face made the commander decide that he would move his troops to the DDR site himself, rather than having them picked up from the bush by the UN. Henri, who was riding along with MONUSCO to pick up the combatants and was unaware of the commander's decision, was called by the Mai Mai and told that the convoy would be shot at if they proceeded further. In the end, Henri was able to defuse an escalating situation, due to his relation with both the Mai Mai group and MONUSCO. Without Henri's relations and knowledge of the situation, this event could have turned deadly. Without the support of outsiders like UN agencies, however, Henri would have had fewer options with which to negotiate with the Mai Mai. In particular, the combination of DDR facilities and services provided by the UN and the facilitation of the process by CRC renders demobilisation a more attractive option for militias.

CRC's contextual and incremental approach in eastern DRC is thus a vital component for both the national and international DDR programmes operating in this region. CRC needs external funding to do its work, but compared to costly[13] international programmes this is a relatively minor investment with great benefits. For example, CRC spends roughly US$153 per former combatant (Gillhespy and Hayman, 2011: 28). This amount excludes the support given by other outsiders, such as the organisations mentioned below. In addition to the support CRC has received from Peace Direct (since 2004) and the Baring Foundation (since 2009), several other examples of the organisation's working relationships with international agencies include:

- Food and Agricultural Organization (FAO): provided seeds, agriculture kits and training in agriculture.
- Handicap International: provided transportation support.
- MONUSCO: joint work on sensitisation of combatants and transport to make contact with militia leaders.
- UNDP: joint training, information sharing, and joint projects on road rehabilitation.
- Save the Children/UNICEF: joint missions to rescue children from the bush.

---

13 *A study done in 2008 calculates the average cost of DDR, based on 19 DDR programmes in 2007, at US$1,434 per person (Escola de Cultura Pau, 2008: 4).*

In effect, CRC operates on a small budget but, in cooperation with outside actors, is able to create tremendous added value for DDR and peacebuilding activities.

Monitoring results and progress

Accurate monitoring of results and the attribution of effects is often much more difficult than evaluators dare to admit. For instance, how is it possible to measure the trust and credibility that has been built up by CRC? How can the potential effects of this trust and credibility for future actions be delineated? How can the precise effects of trust and credibility be measured in relation to past successes and failures? These and many other questions indicate the difficulties of accurately monitoring the results and progress of CRC's work.

Nevertheless, funding and organisational learning require monitoring and evaluation, which CRC mainly does at the community level. In July 2009, for example, the Butembo and Beni Task Forces collaboratively developed indicators for measuring the achievement of CRC's progress in reintegrating ex-combatants.

These indicators were holistic ones that measured the extent of reintegration by how effectively the former combatants became a part of the community: by marrying into the community, building a house, sending their children to school, making a living and believing in black magic. Black magic is an integral part of Mai Mai organisational culture. Hence, measuring whether an ex-combatant continues to believe in black magic (or not) can serve to indicate the distance between former Mai Mai militia members and the rituals of these groups.

Recognising that reintegration also involves action on the part of the community, the task forces included indicators that measured if the community supported the ex-combatants' return. For example, this was done by measuring civilian perceptions of community security in general upon the return of combatants and civilian perspectives on returning combatants in particular. In addition, civilians were also asked what, if any, outside organisations have improved their situation.

The impact of CRC's work

In terms of better understanding the impact of CRC's work, it is important to distinguish between qualitative and quantitative measures of success. It is evident that negotiating and facilitating the return of militia members to their communities entails a high level of dedication and adequate resources before quantifiable results can be evaluated. This labour-intensive work also requires a significant degree of trust and confidence with both militia groups and their local communities, which takes time to grow and develop. However, once trust and confidence are established, this can provide inroads for actions that go beyond the narrowly defined goals related to DDR. For example, in addition to the numbers of people who have gone through a DDR programme or the number of guns collected, trust and confidence can feed into reconciliation and conflict resolution activities, the formation of cooperatives and so on.

Despite these challenges, many quantitative results can be attributed to CRC's work since they began engaging militia groups in 2008. The target of CRC's RDD project was to demobilise 5,000 combatants and give them assistance with reintegration. CRC records currently indicate that 4,305 ex-combatants have been assisted over the past two years. An additional 445 combatants are also expected to be demobilised and reintegrated very soon. Overall, the network of CRC and its local partners now includes six task forces, 18 local peace committees, 24 cooperatives, 119 radio clubs, 16 livelihood projects and 21 families hosting former child soldiers. In addition to its RDD programme, CRC also aimed to assist 2,000 internally displaced persons and facilitate their return. This was greatly exceeded: CRC was able to assist 2,816 families, representing 14,121 persons in all.

CRC has also played a key role in reducing the number of armed militia groups active in North Kivu from nine to four, according to Blaise Kasongo, who manages the organisation's ex-combatants programme (Cairns, 2011: 12). Thanks to CRC's sensitisation work, armed groups have also stopped resisting the return of ex-combatants. At present, several are even negotiating with CRC to help their members leave the bush.

The qualitative impact of CRC's work is perhaps best demonstrated by its six task forces. Whilst the task forces primarily were created to assist in reintegrating ex-combatants and displaced persons, they have now evolved to play many key roles within the community. For example, the task forces have become an authoritative local source of accurate information, including knowledge of other local groups and initiatives working in their communities. In some ways, the task forces have also come to serve as both the community's memory and as a supervisor of the community. The task forces also function as problem solvers called on to deal with a wide variety of community problems. Individual members find their skills as mediators are in demand in resolving disputes. They have become a counter-balance to local government authority, helping to influence the behaviour of elected and appointed officials and hold them to account for their activities. The task forces likewise have become a focal point for local officials, drawing those officials into becoming involved in discussing and addressing the problems of peacebuilding in their communities.

As well as improving community security, these task forces have inspired communities to begin addressing their own economic and social needs through a variety of self-help activities. It is precisely for this reason that at some point friction may develop between CRC's task forces and local governance actors, with governance actors potentially seeing CRC as competition in the future. Thus, the qualitative impact of CRC's work has been to peacefully transform conflicts between returning combatants and recipient communities, to tap into local potentials for conflict transformation, to monitor local dynamics through contextually-devised indicators and to counter rumours by providing verified facts and information.

Testimonies to the impact of CRC

There is ample evidence of the impact of CRC's work from a range of different sources. Butembo-based journalist Edouard Pacifique, for example, views CRC's reintegration activities from a unique perspective.[14] He is a journalist with Radio Moto, which is run by the Catholic diocese of Beni-Butembo. He is also a member of the Butembo Task Force, a record-keeper for CRC and coordinates the radio club network known as 'One for all and all for one', which gathers each Saturday morning at Radio Moto for a two hour call-in show. He says that before Radio Moto and the Catholic

---

14 *The following two paragraphs are largely based on Cairns, 2011: 9.*

diocese decided to work in partnership with CRC, they thoroughly investigated CRC and found it shared the values of the organisation: integrity, faithfulness and a commitment to peace and development.

As a journalist, Pacifique knows many organisations working on demobilisation and claims that CRC's approach is qualitatively different from all the others because they take a more process-oriented and holistic approach to their work. According to Pacifique, CRC's goal is peace and development, unlike other organisations that say 'give me money and then I make demobilisation'. CRC brings a sustained focus and commitment to its work that Pacifique does not see in other such organisations, as he explains:

'They [CRC] are still there since the beginning, compared to other associations that just came and made a broadcast two or three times and then say, no, the project is over, we go, without reporting how many demobilised people they have and what they have done to demobilise them. But with CRC it is quite different, because CRC brings us to where the demobilised are and we see them. CRC shows how they are working there. CRC shows us what it has realised and we see that. That is the difference compared with the other organisations' (Cairns, 2011: 10).

Additional testimony to the effectiveness of CRC's approach comes from the president of radio club Manganga, who is a former combatant. He left the bush as a result of CRC's media sensitisation and now leads a cooperative of ex-combatants that has received support from CRC. He has no regrets, as he says, because CRC has given them 'the radio club and I am doing well and I hope the same for those who still stay there. Thanks to CRC, there is a change of mentality (for the community), a change in their thinking' (*ibid*, 22).

Although he and others had left the bush, this ex-combatant went on to say that he and his demobilised colleagues remain in contact with others who were still there. They had a way of communicating and could meet occasionally, and when they did, the ones in the forest would ask, 'How are you doing? Where you are? And how is the government behaving with you?' If there is no harassment, they are encouraged and decide themselves to leave the bush. As he continued to explain, 'But if they understand things are going wrong, they don't come out and even some who have decided to return will go back to the bush' (*ibid*, 24). He also said that CRC's training sessions on peace and reconciliation helped greatly in building good relationships in the community: 'Every time they are reminding us about good relationships and they keep teaching people about the benefits of living in harmony. As we follow this, we develop such relationships and so we remain in the community without harassment or problems' (*ibid*).

Conclusions and recommendations

Through a relationship with CRC that began in late 2004, Peace Direct has seen CRC develop from an organisation focused on training around 500 displaced people each year in peaceful coexistence with other people in their immediate environment, to an organisation whose mediation skills are called upon by local communities, international NGOs, multilaterals and local government officials across North Kivu.

According to CRC, 'The optimum approach to DDR in DRC has not yet been achieved, but the essential components do exist, if resources and expertise are combined from international, national and local organisations. Organisations should be selected to fulfil particular roles based on cost-effectiveness, sustainability and contextual awareness' (Gillhespy and Hayman, 2011: 32). Creating added value based on actors' various capacities and positions in society is exactly the point when looking for collaboration in the field of DDR. Both insiders and outsiders have (potential) roles defined by strengths and limitations. Only when this is realised and acted upon can substantial improvements in the field of DDR be expected.

Both local populations and outside donors are best served with independent and strategically oriented local NGOs that are prepared to make long-term commitments to the communities in which they work. Although long-term engagement and flexibility are necessary in fragile states, donor logic and management systems often do not allow for this. The success of DDR is, moreover, often measured in numbers of people who have gone through a DDR programme or in the amount of weapons collected. This does not account for questions of outcome and sustainability. Instead, locally appropriate indicators must also be devised together with local NGOs and the intended beneficiaries of any project.

Reintegration efforts should become part and parcel of the design of a DDR programme, and should start even before guns are handed in. It is indeed relevant to consider RDD, rather than DDR, to better highlight the importance of reintegration. CRC experience evidences the need to engage combatants on reintegration immediately after the first contact is made. Not only will this facilitate sustainable reintegration, but it will enhance the likelihood that those militia members who remain in the bush will decide themselves to return to their communities. As the work of CRC has also shown, reintegration efforts should be seen as an opportunity to further the development of entire communities, including embedding local peacebuilding mechanisms in the fabric of their societies.

The distinction made here between a DDR programme and a DDR process is helpful with regard to the complementary roles played by CRC and the international community in the field of DDR. The international community can run a DDR programme that aims to satisfy the needs of a DDR process as much as possible, but requires local initiatives to uncover and address DDR needs from within the local context. Organisations like CRC are capable of creating and sustaining the momentum for peace that is prerequisite for DDR to have a successful and sustainable effect. It is evident that CRC's initiatives are perceived as relevant by local populations because they voluntarily spend large amounts of time and energy on CRC-related work. The international community therefore would be better served in its own DRR aims and objectives to reconsider the ways insiders and outsiders can work together and tailor their collective efforts to local security needs.

References

Alusala, Nelson. Reintegrating Ex-combatants in the Great Lakes Region: Lessons Learned. Monograph 179. Pretoria: Institute for Security Studies, 2011.
Cairns, Rosemary. External Evaluation of Peace Direct and Centre Resolution Conflits Project. Unpublished, 2011.
Escola de Cultura Pau. DDR 2008: Analysis of Disarmament,

Demobilization and Reintegration (DDR) Programmes During 2007. Barcelona: Escola de Cultura Pau, 2008.

Gillhespy, Tom and Carolyn Hayman. Coming Home: A Case Study of Community-led Disarmament, Demobilization and Reintegration in DR Congo. London: Peace Direct, 2011.

Rouw, Hans and Rens C. Willems. Connecting Community Security and DDR: Experiences from Eastern DRC. The Hague: Peace Security and Development Network, 2010.

Rouw, Hans and Rens C. Willems. Unpublished field notes, 2009.

Emphasising reintegration in Burundi: CEDAC

by Rens Willems [1]

The second case study continues in peacebuilding mode, with further attention to reintegrating ex-combatants into their communities. This profile of the Centre d'Encadrement et de Développement des Anciens Combattants (CEDAC) highlights the importance of the self-help elements of Local First. Here, self-help activities occur in a variety of contexts, ranging from peer support groups focused on overcoming the traumas of war, to working cooperatives that create income-generating and livelihood projects, as well as self-funded microcredit schemes. Although CEDAC is locally led, it takes a pragmatic approach to funding by channelling donor support directly to the grassroots through its national network of ex-combatants – a typical locally delivered approach. Nonetheless, this bridging role reflects the value of networking and collaboration that underpins Local First. CEDAC experience also suggests that genuine partnerships between international and local actors require dialogue based on respect for local knowledge about how best to address the challenges a society faces.

'Events that occurred in my life, together with life skills I acquired along the way, inspired me to contribute to the greater good of humanity. May everyone who reads this message be inspired in a similar way to take the opportunity to change the world and make it a better place' (Eric Niragira, www.freewebs.com).

History of conflict in Burundi [2]

Since independence in 1962, Burundi has been plagued by ethnic tensions between the dominant Tutsi minority and the Hutu

---

1 *The author would like to thank CEDAC for its cooperation and for sharing the information necessary for writing this case study. This study is based on several project documents, including: the CEDAC Strategic Plan for 2012-2016, the CEDAC website, and personal communications with Eric Niragira. It also draws on two months of field research on the reintegration of ex-combatants in Burundi in 2010.*
2 *This overview draws from the conflict description in Willems et al, 2010.*

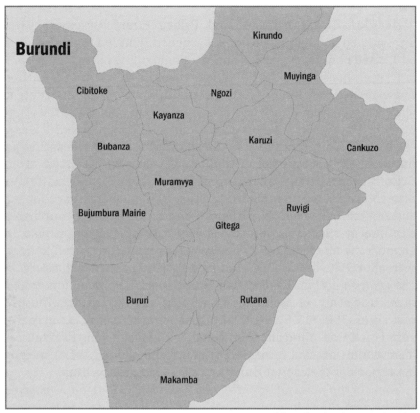

Map showing impact of project

majority.[3] Like Rwanda, which was also colonised by the Germans and since 1916 has been under Belgian tutelage, there were tensions between those groups preceding colonisation. During the colonial period, more dynamic relations between these two groups became frozen and antagonism was fuelled. The Belgian colonisers relied on the Tutsi minority to rule the Hutu majority. They cloaked this arrangement in dubious myths of racial superiority and the traditional domination of the Tutsi over the Hutu, transforming the organisation of society to reflect these myths.[4]

3   *In addition to these two groups, the minority Twa ethnic group comprises about 1 per cent of the population.*
4   *See, for instance: Malkki, L. Purity and Exile: Violence, Memory, and National Cosmology among Hutu Refugees in Tanzania. Chicago & London: The University of Chicago Press, 1995; Prunier, G. The Rwanda Crisis: History of a Genocide. New York: Columbia University Press, 1995; and Reyntjens, F. L'Afrique des Grands Lacs en Crise. Rwanda, Burundi (1988-1994). Paris: Karthala, 1994.*

In 1961, Prime Minister and Prince Louis Rwagasore were assassinated and ethnic tensions sharpened. This led to increasingly ethnicised power struggles within the single ruling party Union pour le Progrès National[5] (UPRONA) and a Tutsi-led coup in the army. Since then, Tutsi minority rule continued almost uninterrupted. Three successive military regimes have been in power and the army became a bastion of Tutsi power. Emerging rebellion met with harsh retaliations from the army, leading to major bloodshed and large outflows of Hutu refugees in 1965, 1972, 1988 and 1991.

Both domestic and international pressure grew, and in 1992 a new constitution providing for multiparty democracy was adopted and military rule came to an end. The first democratic multiparty elections in 1993 were won by Melchior Ndadaye's Front pour la Démocratie au Burundi[6] (FRODEBU), a pro-Hutu party. Shortly thereafter, Ndadaye was assassinated by Tutsi soldiers, which led to revenge killings by FRODEBU members, and a spiral of Tutsi massacres and army reprisals began. The civil war that ensued probably cost some 300,000 lives.[7] In the central parts of the country the population was ethnically segregated, with Tutsi fleeing to displacement camps around local government offices, while whole neighbourhoods of the capital Bujumbura became mono-ethnic.

Some of the political leaders from FRODEBU fled to the exterior and formed the Conseil National pour la Défense de la Démocratie[8] (CNDD), with the Forces pour la Défense de la Démocratie[9] (FDD) as its armed wing, which started attacks on Burundian soil. Another major rebel movement, the Palipehutu-Forces Nationales de Liberation[10] (FNL), was the armed wing of the political party Palipehutu, established in the 1980s in the Tanzanian refugee camps. While Palipehutu-FNL primarily drew support from the central region of Muramvya and along Lake Tanganyika, CNDD was mainly supported in the southern regions of Bururi and Ruyigi. Both movements experienced factional infighting and schism.

In response to the unrest, former military ruler Buyoya staged

---

5 *Union for National Progress.*
6 *Front for Democracy in Burundi.*
7 *Source: BBC News (2012) Burundi Profile. Overview. http://www.bbc.co.uk/news/ world-africa-13085064.*
8 *National Council for the Defence of Democracy.*
9 *Forces for the Defence of Democracy.*
10 *National Forces of Liberation.*

a coup in 1996, thereby suspending the constitution and effectively ending democracy. The coup led to an international boycott that further crippled Burundi's economy. Since 1998, a careful transition towards peace was initiated by Buyoya, who installed a government with more Hutu than Tutsi representatives. After failed talks under the leadership of former Tanzanian President Julius Nyerere in 2001, Nelson Mandela managed to negotiate a transitional government in which Hutu and Tutsi leaders would share power. President Buyoya took up the presidency for the first half of the interim period, after which Domitien Ndayizeye took over. Minister posts in this period were divided equally among the two ethnicities.

However, the main Hutu rebel groups CNDD-FDD and the Palipehutu-FNL refused to sign the ceasefire and fighting continued. Only towards the end of 2003 was agreement reached between the government and the CNDD-FDD. FDD leader Pierre Nkurunziza, and other FDD members, received some ministerial appointments. In 2004, a UN peacekeeping force took over from African Union troops and a disarmament and demobilisation programme started. A new national army was to be formed, incorporating former government soldiers and former fighters of the CNDD-FDD.

In 2005, in the first democratic elections since the civil war, the CNDD-FDD won parliamentary elections, and Nkurunziza was elected president. Most ministerial posts were in the hands of the CNDD-FDD, although FRODEBU and UPRONA also became part of the government. The inauguration of Nkurunziza implied an end to the transitional period. Nkurunziza promoted a policy of unity and reconciliation, and hoped to encourage the return of refugees from exile. He also took a conciliatory stance towards the FNL, and at the end of 2006, a ceasefire was signed with the government. The truce had to overcome several hurdles, including clashes between rival FNL factions in Bujumbura and raids in the northwest of the country, until the end of 2008, when a peace agreement was signed. FNL leadership returned from exile in Tanzania and the movement was officially transformed into a political party.

Since mid-2008, no large-scale security incidents have occurred. In January 2009, civil war was officially declared to be ended. Nonetheless, especially since the 2010 elections, political tensions have remained high between the CNDD, which controls the government, and opposition parties.

CEDAC background

It is in the above-described context that CEDAC developed as an organisation. Founded in 2005 in Bujumbura, CEDAC is a local and apolitical non-profit organisation.[11] Today, CEDAC has a managing board consisting of eight people, all of whom are Burundian nationals, and includes a national network of 129 local committees at the communal level and 18 committees at provincial levels. The organisation and its mission started with its founding president, Eric Niragira. When Melchior Ndadaye was assassinated in 1993 and the Burundian civil war started, Eric was 14 years old. The school he attended closed, as did many other schools in the country, and people of all ages were drawn into the conflict that quickly spread throughout the country. Like many young Hutus at the time, Eric was forced to support the rebellion. Put under pressure by people within the rebel movements, he officially joined the CNDD in 1994 and participated in its military and political activities. During this time, several of his family members fled the country, whilst Eric stayed with his younger sister and his younger brother.

Separated from their family, they went back to secondary school in 1996. However, the conflict continued and further sharpened divisions between Hutus and Tutsis. His class was predominantly Tutsi, making school a difficult and painful experience, as he explains:

> 'On a daily basis, the army would gather fellow Tutsi students to participate in the killing of civilians who lived in the villages surrounding our lycee. When these students would return, the Hutu students were forced to wash their clothing and knives that were full of blood. We did this out of fear of being killed if we refused' (ibid).

During Christmas in 1996, Eric tried to return to his village to meet some family members, which was only four kilometres away. Halfway he encountered people fleeing, who warned him that the army was killing people in his village. He nonetheless continued, but just before he arrived he saw soldiers burning houses and killing people. Eric quickly returned to his school, finding dead bodies and burned houses along the way:

---

11 *This description is based on the CEDAC website: http://www.freewebs.com/cedac/biographyoftheauthor.htm.*

'In lycee, every night before I would go to bed I took the time to think about the countless events I witnessed during war. People killed in my own village, women raped, explosions, my family in exile, and my own precarious situation. I started to think about what I could do to help my people to survive and to make a change in my country. I decided that I would continue supporting the rebellion movement in a positive way by mobilizing students and civilians to support the movement politically' (ibid).

While Eric occasionally would participate in attacks on army positions, he was mainly active in sensitisation work about the vision the rebels had for the country.

He later came into contact with the Centre Indépendant de Recherche et d'Initiative pour le Dialogue (CIRID),[12] a Geneva-based NGO founded by a Burundian national, which aimed to support the consolidation of peace in the African Great Lakes Region, and Burundi in particular. Eric became an international youth group leader for CIRID, which brought him into contact with other young people from the Great Lakes Region. This stimulated him to discuss and think about the ways in which he, and other youth like him, could play a role in peacebuilding. When CIRID wanted to recruit 24 locals for an externally funded project, hundreds of ex-combatants from the conflict that had just ended showed up looking for work. Having participated in the conflict himself, Eric started to think about how ex-combatants could be supported. He shared his thoughts with some of his friends, where he found support for his ideas. Together with eight other people, Eric founded a new organisation with the aim of supporting ex-combatants, as well as the people of Burundi as a whole, in the development of the country. Thus the Centre d'Encadrement et de Développement des Anciens Combattants (CEDAC) was born.

The issue

CEDAC originated in response to the lack of reintegration of many ex-combatants in post-conflict Burundi, and the continuing presence of armed violence. At the individual level, many ex-combatants in

---

12 *Independent Centre for Research and Initiatives for Dialogue.*

Burundi had relatively little free choice when they joined an armed group or militia force because there was considerable pressure on young people to support the struggle – from both sides of the conflict. From the perspective of many civilians, however, ongoing insecurity is associated with the presence of ex-combatants in their communities. Civilians have indicated that they are afraid of ex-combatants because of their actual or suspected past involvement in human rights violations, pillage and/or theft in the very communities in which they are now reintegrated. In some cases, local residents have also experienced harassment by ex-combatants, who regard themselves of a higher status than everyday citizens because they fought for the interests of their country. As a result, ex-combatants are often feared and marginalised.

A survey undertaken by Oxfam Novib in the Netherlands, for example, showed that 80 per cent of the people interviewed perceived ex-combatants as a threat to security.[13] And during field research in 2010, it came out that ex-combatants were mistrusted, and communities often linked crime and insecurity to the presence of ex-combatants. Demobilised combatants are often thought to be involved in armed robberies, theft and political violence, with some interviewees offering highly specific examples of the role of ex-combatants in criminal behaviour in their communities. While some ex-combatants do commit crimes, many of them do not. Nonetheless, ex-combatants as a whole are often pointed to as the source of crime.

At the same time, the communities to which ex-combatants returned also had expectations. For example, sometimes ex-combatants were expected to bring home financial gains as a result of receiving financial assistance through the Burundian disarmament, demobilisation and reintegration (DDR) programme. Such expectations were raised further when others in the community

---

13 *International NGO meeting, Bujumbura, 17 June 2010. It should be noted that during the same meeting it was mentioned that in a survey of the Norwegian Refugee Council (NRC), the majority of returning refugees and internally displaced persons (IDPs) did not see ex-combatants as a security threat to them. This difference could be explained by the fact that the survey of the NRC focused on IDPs and refugees, and the survey of Oxfam Novib included community members who stayed in Burundi during the war, and arguably witnessed the violence of ex-combatants in more direct ways, whereas refugees were in camps out of reach of the violence. In interviews from 2010, it was found that many community members accuse ex-combatants of the crimes currently being committed in their communities, and thus see them as a security threat.*

heard of the financial support ex-combatants had received. In other communities, those ex-combatants who had received support through the DDR programme were excluded from community development projects and related employment opportunities. In yet other circumstances, when coming back to their communities without any benefits, either for their families or their wider community, as well as lacking capacities to find work and make an economic contribution to the betterment of their communities, ex-combatants were considered useless or even a burden. In such cases, as one analyst comments, 'Ironically, a programme that has been designed to facilitate cohabitation between demobilised and the rest of the population seems to have the opposite effect' (Geenen, 2008: 137).[14]

In short, ineffective economic reintegration can lead to stigmatisation of ex-combatants and obstruct social reintegration. For instance, as a community member in Kibemba explained:

> *'In Burundi it is normal for people to think bad things of people who do not work or go to school. Ex-combatants often do not have any work and when there are problems they are indeed often suspect. When they returned they fell into a situation where they have nothing to do. So when there is crime, people think it was them because they have nothing [to do] on their hands' (Group discussion, Kibimba, Gitega, 9 June 2010).*

Thus, when ex-combatants have trouble reintegrating, this increases perceptions that they are dependent, a burden to communities, and responsible for violence and crime.

The failure of economic and social reintegration into civilian life also creates the risk that ex-combatants may be tempted to return to arms. Peace is especially fragile in the period immediately after a settlement has been reached. For example, the World Bank (2004: 8) found that post-conflict countries face a 44 per cent chance of reverting to conflict within the first five years, and Paul Collier (2003: 7) and his colleagues argue that half of post-conflict countries return to conflict within the decade. Experts

---

14 *Translated from the original French: 'Ironiquement, un programme qui a été conçu pour faciliter la cohabitation entre les démobilisés et le reste de la population semble avoir des effets opposés.'*

on peacebuilding have therefore indicated that 'the successful disarmament, demobilisation and reintegration (DDR) of former combatants after violent conflict represents the touchstone, the moment of truth, for any peacebuilding process' (Salomons, 2005: 19). While the costs of demobilisation and reintegration may be high, according to Kingma:

'Long-term costs for society – or even the region – could be larger if the ex-combatants were unable to find new livelihoods. It could lead to increasing unemployment and social deprivation, which could again lead to rising crime rates and political instability' (Kees Kingma, 2000: 19).

Furthermore, once a peace agreement has been signed, violence generally continues in the post-settlement period. In Burundi, political tensions have remained high and there have been numerous violent incidents. In particular, criminality rates are high and (armed) robbery and burglary were reported by communities as the most common security problems (Willems et al, 2010: 30-32). In part, this is due to the proliferation of small arms and light weapons in Burundi, which feeds criminality, causes continued fear and distrust – particularly in those communities where violence had strong ethnic dimensions – and enables small fights to quickly escalate into larger-scale conflicts. It is often joked that a grenade, a weapon commonly used in Burundi, is about the same price as a large bottle of beer.[15]

The development of CEDAC

When CEDAC was founded, there was no funding to initiate activities. But by organising ex-combatants and other survivors of the conflict into a network, CEDAC provided them with a platform where they could discuss their grievances and problems, as well as find ways in which they could help one another. CEDAC focused on this particular target group because they not only could potentially

---

15 *Mentioned during various discussions with communities in Burundi during field research in 2010. Further research revealed that a grenade costs around US$4, which is the equivalent of four large bottles of beer.*

cause insecurity, but as the majority of them were young, this group could also serve the development of the country. In Eric's words:

'I became witness to bloody events that claimed many innocent lives. I began to question and eventually believe that the immense destruction I saw daily also harnessed the power to rebuild in the form of peace' (CEDAC website: http://www.freewebs.com/cedac/biographyoftheauthor.htm).

The first initiative undertaken by CEDAC and its network members was a sensitisation campaign promoting civilian disarmament in order to directly address the proliferation of weapons and the armed violence this caused in Burundi. At the same time, ex-combatants became a frontrunner of the peace process, demonstrating their good intentions by voluntarily promoting disarmament. This also supported their reintegration as it helped build confidence and showed communities that these ex-combatants were working for peace and stability. During the campaign, more than 500 weapons and several thousands of rounds of ammunition were collected by members of CEDAC. These weapons were voluntarily handed in by ex-combatants and other community members and then turned over to the government (CEDAC Project Proposal, no date: 3).

The campaign likewise showed the potential for ex-combatants from the different armed factions of the past conflict to work together toward a common goal. This motivated CEDAC to continue and expand its activities. Consequently, CEDAC facilitated the formation of provincial and communal committees all across the country.[16] In 2005, a total of 129 committees were formed at the communal level and 18 at the provincial level. Today an estimated 60 per cent of these groups continue to actively engage in activities, which primarily aim to coordinate the activities of CEDAC and help ex-combatants support one another in their reintegration. These committees consist of ex-combatants who are elected by their peers for a period of four years.

In this framework, the members of CEDAC are supported with their social and economic reintegration through capacity building

---

16 *Provincial committees are composed of three people, including at least one woman; communal committees are composed of five people, including at least two women (CEDAC Strategic Plan, no date: 5-6).*

activities, such as vocational training and peer-to-peer support, to transform their spirits of war and promote local development initiatives (CEDAC Project Proposal, no date: 2). Committee members are encouraged to start income generating activities in cooperation with one another and contribute small amounts of funds for their own microcredit projects. Several associations (a term commonly used in Burundi to refer to small working cooperatives) have been formed, many of which also include other members of the community. These associations have created, for instance, farming cooperatives, rice plantations and small businesses.

CEDAC does not receive external funding for this work, but instead primarily plays a motivational support role to encourage its committees to start these types of working cooperatives together. Importantly, CEDAC also recommends that other community members be included in these cooperatives as this can help facilitate reintegration of ex-combatants into their communities. Some of these associations have received material support and training through CEDAC's implementation of external partner programmes.

CEDAC partnerships

CEDAC has developed a range of different partnerships and collaborations with other Burundian civil society organisations and various international organisations.[17] This has facilitated the sharing of information and experiences at both national and international levels on the reintegration of ex-combatants, the reduction of armed violence and the collection of weapons and ammunition. Importantly, these collaborations have also enabled CEDAC to channel support from international donors directly to ex-combatants in Burundi. In particular, CEDAC uses its organisational structure to tender for

---

17 *These include, amongst others, Action on Armed Violence (AOAV), BIRATURABA, Borderpol, Burundian Vision, Centre d'Alerte et de Prévention des Conflits (CENAP), Centre indépendant de Recherches et d'Initiatives pour le Dialogue (CIRID), Centre for International Conflict Analysis and Management (CICAM), Center for International Stabilization and Recovery (CISR), Cluster Munitions Coalition (CMC), UN Food and Agriculture Organization (FAO), International Action Network on Small Arms (IANSA), International Campaign to Ban Landmines (ICBL), Institute for Security Studies (ISS), Ligue Iteka, Peace Direct, Mine Action Canada (MAC), Réseau Communautaire pour l'Assistance des Victimes de la Guerre (RECOVI), Small Arms Survey, Survivor Corps, UNDP and UNIFEM.*

donor projects, which it implements through its extensive network.

For example, with the support of the United Nations Food and Agriculture Organization (FAO), CEDAC distributed seeds and fertiliser in Muramvya Province to ex-combatants, who used them to start up their local cooperative farming activities.

In conjunction with the United Nations Development Fund for Women (UNIFEM), CEDAC led an initiative to establish a national structure composed of committees at the local, provincial and national levels. Membership of these committees consists of female ex-combatants and women associated with the armed forces.[18] These women were trained on how to organise and manage their committees, as well as learned about processes related to creating social cohesion and UN resolution 1325.[19] At present, the national structure still exists and functions in cooperation with the other committees that belong to the CEDAC network (CEDAC Rapport Final du Projet, no date: 2-3). Moreover, in cooperation with a variety of organisations, CEDAC has been working on the issue of gender-based violence by strengthening the voice of women and talking with men about the views of women and their position in society, and advocating emancipation and equality.

With CARE, Survivor Corps and the Centre for International Stabilization and Recovery, in 2007 CEDAC organised trainings for female ex-combatants on peer-to-peer support in the provinces of Bujumbura Mairie, Bujumbura Rural, Cibitoke, Muramvya and Bubanza. These provinces were chosen because of the heavy military activity that took place there, and because this is where the war lasted for the longest time. During these trainings, female ex-combatants learned how to support one another in dealing with traumas from the war. This is a very effective way to support trauma healing and social reintegration in a country like Burundi, where psycho-social support is very limited.[20] CEDAC has future plans to organise similar trainings for male ex-combatants, which will build

---

18 *There is a committee of five women's representatives at the national level, provincial committees consisting of three women, and communal committees with five representatives.*
19 *Resolution 1325 seeks to increase the participation of women in all levels of peace negotiations and peacebuilding, and calls for attention to the specific needs of girls and women in conflict, transitional and post-conflict settings.*
20 *During the 2010 field research, limited psycho-social support was mentioned in several interviews with representatives of local NGOs, international NGOs, donors and the national government.*

on the work the organisation has already done to encourage them to share their experiences and support one another; eg, the peer-to-peer support elements of the provincial and communal committees that CEDAC has established throughout Burundi.

Several CEDAC projects have secured funding from the United Nations Development Program (UNDP), the first of which was a campaign to stop armed violence and promote civilian disarmament in 2008. A more recent programme involved men and women associated with the FNL, referred to as Adultes Associés,[21] in the provinces of Bujumbura Rural, Bubanza and Cibitoke. People could apply to participate in work crews composed of 20 ex-combatants and ten members from the local communities to take part in cash-for-work projects, such as the construction of houses, school buildings, and roads and bridges. These cash-for-work projects lasted about three months, during which time the workers received a salary and were asked to save one third of this for the next phase of the programme. Those who wanted could then participate in the second phase, whereby they were expected to contribute their savings from the previous phase. UNDP quadrupled the amounts that each group had saved, the additional funds from which were then used by the groups to start up livelihood projects, like small businesses or farming. Those who chose to continue could propose their own plans for their livelihood project. UNDP supported these proposals, as well as reviewed their feasibility. During the second phases of these projects, CEDAC helped organise a total of 41 associations and provided them with the support and training they needed to succeed in their business ventures.[22]

Reintegrating ex-combatants in Burundi: outside interventions and local efforts

The process of reintegrating ex-combatants in Burundi has also been undertaken through outside interventions. When the first

---

21 *The Adultes Associés are both men and women that supported the FNL in various ways, such as transportation of materials, weapons and ammunition, hiding combatants, cooking, etc. Although they generally did not participate in direct combat, they perceive themselves to be ex-combatants.*
22 *This amounts to a total of 1,230 people who have been organised in associations through CEDAC efforts.*

peace agreements were signed in 2004, this included the formation of new state security forces, which were composed of members from both the former army and the rebel forces. However, the total combined number of the armed forces and rebel groups was too large. Consequently, surplus soldiers and combatants went through a disarmament, demobilisation and reintegration (DDR) programme as part of the World Bank's Multi-country Demobilisation and Reintegration Program (MDRP), which was to demobilise a total of about 78,000 ex-combatants (Escola de Cultura de Pau, 2008: 4).

Once people volunteered or were selected for demobilisation, they were disarmed in their barracks and transported to the demobilisation centre, where their status was formally changed to civilian. During their stay in the demobilisation camp, ex-combatants received training on a variety of topics. After being discharged from the camp, they received a reinsertion package, which equalled 18 months of salary and consisted of a minimum total amount of 566,000 fbu (roughly US$515), depending on military rank. This reinsertion package was paid in four separate instalments. The first was paid in cash at the demobilisation centre, with the remainder paid out through the banking system in their community of choice over a ten month period (Boshoff and Vrey, 2006: 22).

After this, demobilised combatants had five options with regard to their reintegration support:

1. Return to former employment situation (re-employment).
2. Go back to formal education.
3. Engage in vocational training.
4. Receive entrepreneurial support.
5. Receive Income-Generating Activities support.[23]

The large majority of ex-combatants opted for the last option, which included goods of their choice (for example, food items for trade, animals, equipment, etc.) with a value of 600,000 fbu (roughly US$545); they had also received information on how to set up a small business project whilst at the demobilisation site (Douma and Gasana, 2008: 6). This choice was preferred because ex-combatants expected that it would provide fast revenue, and because vocational training was considered too expensive.[24] Despite a system of focal

---

23 *This programme was similar to the one that was subsequently implemented in 2008 for demobilised FLN combatants.*
24 *Many ex-combatants could not afford to travel to or live in Bujumbura, where most*

points (ie, ex-combatants who represented the ex-combatants in their communities at provincial and national levels) and the free choice to determine which reintegration kit they wanted, many ex-combatants felt that they were not sufficiently involved in the execution of the programme, including decision making. The programme also suffered many delays caused by capacity problems, corruption on the side of the Burundian government and the bureaucracy associated with international assistance from large organisations like the World Bank.

In particular, the delayed payment of benefits to ex-combatants was the cause of several mass demonstrations in front of the national DDR office by protesting ex-combatants. These delays also gave some ex-combatants the impression that the DDR process 'was only there to excommunicate [sic] us from the armed groups'.[25] Frustrations such as these can potentially cause problems, among other things because they can increase the susceptibility of the ex-combatants to political manipulation and incline them to return to violence. As one ex-combatant sums up the situation,

> 'After all the fighting, it is hard to go back into civilian life. I realise that life was much easier as a combatant. Of course it was hard, but at least I had food and could drink whenever I wanted. Now I sometimes think to pick up a weapon again' (Interview with ex-combatant FNL, Kabezi, Bujumbura Rurale, 28 April 2010).

Clearly, the benefits provided through the national DDR programme offered ex-combatants a significant income boost (Gilligan et al, forthcoming: 1). However, it is problematic that there is little evidence of a sustained effect of these external programmes on the social and economic reintegration of ex-combatants. For example, a World Bank report on selected components of the DDR programme in Burundi finds the success of economic reintegration to be uneven, and establishes that only two per cent of the ex-combatants were able to satisfy six basic needs.[26] Quantitative studies

---

vocational training programmes are located.
25 *Interview with ex-combatant Ex-FAB, Muyinga, Muyinga, conducted 11 May 2010.*
26 *According to a World Bank (2009: 19) report, these six basic needs included access to potable water, decent housing, adequate clothing, eating at least twice a day, children's education, and healthcare. Fifty-five per cent could satisfy one of these needs, 22 per cent*

assessing reintegration in Sierra Leone and Liberia point out that the economic impact of DDR reintegration support is limited or non-existent.[27] As discussed above, if ex-combatants fail to successfully reintegrate into civilian life, this may lead to increased security problems. A study on the DDR programme for paramilitary groups in Colombia, for instance, finds that the programme did appear to have reduced homicidal violence, but that these results also disappeared over time (Restrepo and Muggah, 2009: 40).

The reason why it is so difficult for international interventions to have a sustained effect on the reintegration of ex-combatants is that reintegration is a complex national and local process. At best, outside interventions can only exert a positive influence on these processes. However, they are often limited by time constraints and lack of knowledge about the local context and processes on the ground.

This is why the work of local organisations like CEDAC is pivotal. CEDAC did not have the resources or the organisational capacity to roll out the DDR programme that was undertaken by the World Bank. Right after the signing of the peace agreement, the World Bank funded the provision of benefits to sustain thousands of former combatants who suddenly had nothing to do. In a situation of fragile peace, outside interventions like this bought time and supported the initial steps of the reintegration process. But the process of reintegrating ex-combatants into communities and taking up civilian life is a long-term undertaking. In contrast, the programmes of external interventions can only support this for so long. It is the Burundian people who must continue this process. It is therefore only through the efforts of the individuals in communities, who are supporting one another through associations and committees with the help of CEDAC, that the results of these outside interventions can be sustained. In other words, when outside interveners pack their bags, CEDAC will remain and continue to support ex-combatants in their long-term reintegration process. Local organisations like CEDAC also thoroughly understand the local contexts where they work, which is necessary for adapting programmes and

---

could cover two, and 14 per cent could cover four. Only two per cent could cover all.
27 For Sierra Leone, see for example: Humphreys, M. and J. M. Weinstein. 'Demobilization and Reintegration', Journal of Conflict Resolution, 51(4), 2007, pages 531-567. For Liberia, see for example: Levely, quoted in Gilligan, M, E Mvukiyehe and C Samii. 'Reintegrating rebels into civilian life: Quasi-experimental evidence from Burundi', Journal of Conflict Resolution, forthcoming, page 5.

projects to the conditions on the ground. Moreover, large networks on the ground, such as the ones CEDAC has built over time, are helpful for the implementation of projects at the community level.

There are also crucial differences between CEDAC's approach and those of outside interveners. For instance, outside support generally has strict target groups and regions for purposes of manageability; eg, support for ex-combatants who handed in a weapon comes from the World Bank, support for the Adultes Associés from UNDP and support for women comes from UNIFEM. For CEDAC, in contrast, it is not only those who carried a weapon who matter, but all of those who participated, voluntarily or by force, in any way in supporting the armed forces and rebel militia groups. Because its mission is to support the reintegration of ex-combatants and the development of Burundi, CEDAC prioritises inclusion. At times, this is difficult: donors often want to support a project for a particular target population that is narrowly defined, but CEDAC aims to support a much broader group. Differentiated support, creating differences in what groups get what kind of support and when, can be contradictory to the ultimate goal of reintegrating ex-combatants and bringing communities together.

Conclusion

One of the strengths of CEDAC is that the organisation integrates the different elements of outside interventions by bringing a large group of ex-combatants together in a national network and channelling the different projects proposed by outside donors to them. CEDAC also creates and supports the sustainability of the effects outside interventions aim to have and broadens their potential impact. For instance, where peer-to-peer trainings are given to a particular group, CEDAC promotes what it has learned from these experiences to groups across the country.

However, serving as an implementation partner for outside interveners also creates the risk that CEDAC loses its own vision and approach. Realising this, CEDAC has recently developed a strategic plan for the coming years, which is oriented to maintaining its own focus and mission. While this mission is broadly supported, so far it has proven difficult to find funding. Outside organisations and donors often have their own projects and ideas, as well as considerably more influence on how and where funds are spent. CEDAC's response to recent challenges in securing funds to implement its strategic plan is to improve its advocacy capacities. At the same time, outside organisations working with local NGOs as implementing partners should realise that a genuine partnership works both ways, which necessitates dialogue about how to support the mission of its local partners.

Recommendations

1. For successful reintegration of ex-combatants, the involvement of local communities is vital, and local organisations can play a key role in connecting outside interventions to them.
2. Be more responsive to local differences and be open for local initiatives. Realise that such local initiatives could do a lot with relatively little money, if given the opportunity.
3. When using local organisations as implementing partners, see how the partnership can also support the mission of these local organisations.

References

Boshoff, H. and W. Vrey. A Technical Analysis of Disarmament, Demobilisation and Reintegration. A Case Study from Burundi. ISS Monograph series, No 125. Pretoria: Institute for Security Studies, 2006.

CEDAC, Project Proposal. 'Projet d'appui à la réintégration durable des ex-combattants au Burundi. Présentation de l'organisation soumissionnaire', no date.

CEDAC, Rapport Final du Projet, no date.

CEDAC, Strategic Plan 2012-2016. Bujumbura: CEDAC, no date.

Collier, P., L. Elliott, H. Hegre, A. Hoeffler, M. Reynal-Querol, N. Sambanis. Breaking the Conflict Trap: Civil War and Development Policy. Washington D.C.: World Bank, 2003.

Douma, P. and J. M. Gasana. Reintegration in Burundi: Between

Happy Cows and Lost Investments. The Hague: Netherlands Institute for International Relations Clingendael, 2008.

Escola de Cultura de Pau. Burundi. Barcelona: Escola de Cultura de Pau, 2008.

Geenen, S. 'Les Combattants au Carrefour. La Réintégration Socio-économique des Ex-combattants au Burundi et en RDC' in S. Marysse, F. Reyntjens and S.Vandeginste (eds.) *L'Afrique des Grands Lacs. Annuaire 2007-2008. Paris: l'Harmattan, 2008.*

Gilligan, M., E. Mvukiyehe and C. Samii. 'Reintegrating Rebels into Civilian Life: Quasi-experimental Evidence from Burundi', *Journal of Conflict Resolution, forthcoming.*

Kingma, K. (ed.). *Demobilization in Sub-Saharan Africa. The Development and Security Impacts. London: McMillan Press Ltd, 2000.*

Restrepo, J.A. and R. Muggah. 'Colombia's Quiet Demobilization: A Security Dividend?' in Muggah, R. (ed.). *Security and Post-Conflict Reconstruction: Dealing with Fighters in the Aftermath of War. New York: Routledge, 2009.*

Salomons, D. 'Security: An Absolute Prerequisite' in G. Junne and W. Verkoren (eds.), *Postconflict Development: Meeting New Challenges. London: Lynne Rienner Publishers, 2005.*

Willems, R., J. Kleingeld and M. van Leeuwen. *Connecting Community Security and DDR: Experiences from Burundi. The Hague: Peace, Security and Development Network, 2010.*

World Bank. *Rapport de Mise en Œuvre et Résultats d'un Don de l'IDA pour un Projet d'Urgence de Démobilisation, Réinsertion et Réintégration. ICR1152, 2009.*

World Bank. *The Role of the World Bank in Conflict and Development: An Evolving Agenda. Washington DC: World Bank, 2004.*

Collecting the artefacts of war in Mozambique: FOMICRES

by Mairéad Heffron [1]

Bringing the peacebuilding focus of the first half of this volume to a close, the third case study emphasises the broad range of cross-cutting relationships between civil society and government that can make for an effective Local First approach. Focused on the collection of small arms and light weapons and other artefacts of war in Mozambique, the work of the Força Moçambicana para Investigação de Crimes e Reinserção Social (FOMICRES) goes even further: it demonstrates the potential for inter-state cooperation on security issues and the valuable role that locally led civil society organisations can play in accessing information about weapons caches at the community level. As with the other two case studies, trust and local knowledge are essential for success. Describing the genesis of FOMICRES, this case study shows how locally led organisations change over time and develop new capacities to better respond to their own dynamic contexts. It also delineates the critical factors necessary to draw relevant cost comparisons of different weapons collection projects.

Context

Background to the conflict

A Portuguese colony for almost five centuries, Mozambique gained independence in 1974 after a ten year liberation struggle. This armed struggle was led by the Front for the Liberation of Mozambique (FRELIMO), and in 1975, FRELIMO's president Samora Machel was sworn in as president of the new People's Republic of Mozambique. A Marxist-Leninist one-party state model was adopted and the republic had support from countries such as the USSR.

The new state faced numerous challenges at this point and the government adopted a number of political and military strategies that did not serve to lighten the burden (Morgan, 1990: 610).[2] Firstly,

---

1 *The author wishes to thank all of her interview partners for their cooperation and assistance in providing valuable information and insights for this case study.*
2 *Morgan describes the strategies that were adopted as 'spectacularly misguided'.*

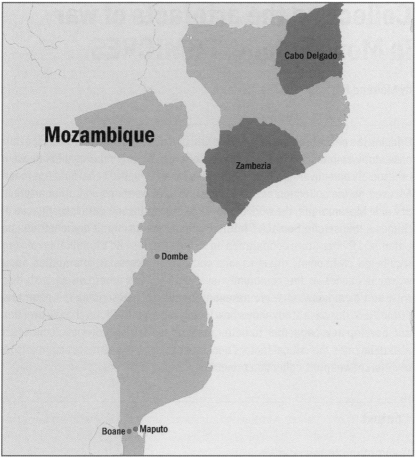

Map showing impact of project

being suspicious of those who had fought on the side of the enemy in the liberation war, no attempts were made by the government to integrate soldiers from the colonial government's army into the armed forces of the new state. At the same time, FRELIMO's own armed forces were 'largely undisciplined, uneducated and underpaid' (Berman, 1999: 13), and there was much dissatisfaction within these forces with austerity measures introduced by Machel.

Secondly, as a UN member state, the FRELIMO government took the decision in 1976 to honour a UN security council resolution requesting member states to embargo trade with white-minority ruled Rhodesia.[3] Not only did this prevent landlocked Rhodesia

---

3 *See resolution 253 (1968): http://www.un.org/documents/sc/res/1968/scres68.htm.*

from accessing Mozambique ports, but it created problems for many Mozambicans whose livelihoods were tied up in that same trade (*ibid*). In addition to the trade embargo, Mozambique showed its dissatisfaction with the Rhodesian regime in other ways. Namely, the Machal government provided logistical and material support to the Zimbabwe African National Liberation Army (ZANLA), the military wing of the Zimbabwe African National Union (ZANU), and allowed ZANLA to operate from within Mozambican territory.

Rhodesia fought back by providing support to the establishment of the Mozambique National Resistance (Resistência Nacional Moçambicana, or RENAMO), which was comprised of those people dissatisfied with the FRELIMO government, including ex-soldiers. Later, the South Africa government also lent support to the RENAMO forces in Mozambique.[4] In turn, FRELIMO appealed to East Germany and the Soviet Union for assistance, and thus from 1976-1977 there ensued a conflict that continued into the 1990s. The changing regional and global political climate in the late 1980s and early 1990s saw a reduction in outside military support for both sides involved in the conflict and as a result (combined with the protracted nature of the conflict, which eventually took its toll on both sides), the first steps towards peace became possible.

The peace accord (General Peace Agreement)

The peace process in Mozambique was the result of a long negotiation process led by church partners of both Catholic and Protestant denominations, such as the Christian Council of Mozambique. By the late 1980s, these church partners had become increasingly concerned with the effects of the war on the general population. Drought had also become an issue in southern and central areas. The resulting famine and the prolonged civil war caused thousands of deaths and displaced hundreds of thousands of people.

In particular, the Christian Council of Mozambique played an important role in raising national and international awareness of the humanitarian crisis in the country. Locally, it educated people on the need for peace, linking peace to bible passages during homilies, etc. The council also received support on mediation, including training, from the World Council of Churches and the All Africa Conference of Churches. A Peace and Reconciliation Commission

---

4 See: http://www.iss.co.za/af/profiles/Mozambique/Politics.html.

was established and carried out training in communities. Church networks were used to facilitate initial discussions with the rebels (see Murdock and Zunguza, 2010). Eventually and initially in secret, Joaquim Chissano, Machel's successor (Machel was killed in an airplane crash in South Africa in 1986), began to discuss the role that church leaders could play in contacting the RENAMO forces. The Community of Sant' Egidio, a Catholic lay organisation based in Rome but with strong humanitarian ties to Mozambique, also played an important mediation role, and was a signatory to the final accord. The result of all these efforts was that in Rome in October 1992, Chissano and Dhlakama, the leader of RENAMO, signed a peace accord marking the end of 16 years of war.

United Nations operation in Mozambique

Under the 1992 peace agreement, both parties agreed to a ceasefire, demobilisation of armed troops and militia (RENAMO) forces and multiparty elections.[5] A Security Council resolution passed in December of that year established the United Nations Operation in Mozambique, ONUMOZ[6] (also known as UNAMOZ). The mandate of ONUMOZ was to monitor the implementation of the peace agreement, including supporting the election process and overseeing the disarmament and demobilisation of troops. Due to delays, however, the mission was only deployed in its full capacity eight months after the peace agreement was signed. ONUMOZ also coordinated and monitored humanitarian assistance efforts.

Elections were held in October 1994, in which FRELIMO won a majority of votes and Joaquim Chissano was re-elected as president. ONUMOZ remained until December 1994, having overseen the demobilisation of 80,000 troops, the formation of the new national defence force, Forças Armadas de Defesa de Moçambique (FADM), consisting of 12,000 troops, and the collection of almost 200,000 weapons from military and paramilitary forces. Some of these weapons were destroyed and the remainder were handed over to FADM. Although ONUMOZ made great strides in ensuring the peace agreement was implemented, when the mission was dissolved,

---

5 *For an electronic version of the peace agreement, see: http://www.usip.org/publications/peace-agreements-mozambique.*
6 *Security Council Resolution 797 S/RES/797 1992: http://www.un.org/documents/sc/res/1992/scres92.htm.*

serious issues remained about the number of weapons in-country. ONUMOZ's final report expressed concerns about safekeeping of weapons handed to FADM and widespread arms caches.[7]

The issue

When ONUMOZ forces entered Mozambique, very little was definitely known about the number of weapons present. Some reports state that the estimated number of arms distributed to civilians by FRELIMO and RENAMO during the conflict was close to 1.5 million (see Leão, 2004a). Other estimates put the number of AK47s in the country in 1995 at 6 million, including AK47s held by the armed forces (see Smith, 1999). According to some sources, lack of knowledge regarding the number of weapons brought into the country by RENAMO was a major constraint to making accurate estimates. Evidence also suggests that the records maintained by the FRELIMO government were not very accurate either (see Faltas and Paes, 2004). According to reports, records and information on the number and types of weapons and ammunition were either non-existent or unavailable to ONUMOZ. As a result, the number of weapons voluntarily handed over or uncovered in the latter phase of operations 'represented only a token gesture' (Berman, 1991: 2). On top of this, only a small number of weapons handed over to ONUMOZ were destroyed. The ONUMOZ final mission report states:

> 'A limited amount of arms, ammunition and explosives was destroyed, whilst the remainder was transferred to the new Mozambican Defence Force (FADM). There is concern about their safe keeping and I very much hope that the Government of Mozambique will take all necessary measures in that regard as soon as possible, destroying or otherwise disposing of all weapons that will not be needed for the FADM and the national police' (Boutros-Ghali, 1994: 3).

For whatever reason, an unspecified number of arms remained in the country after ONUMOZ left. The concerns highlighted in the

---

7 For a full version of the ONUMOZ final report, see: http://daccess-dds-ny.un.org/doc/ UNDOC/GEN/N94/515/76/PDF/N9451576.pdf?OpenElement.

Interview with former Small Arms Advisor, UNDP Mozambique

'Various reasons are put forward as to why people held on to weapons after the conflict, and these reasons vary, depending on whether the weapons were retained by an individual/household or by those armed groups actively involved in the conflict. Some people or households may have kept a weapon as a means of personal defence from thieves, wild animals, etc. Others probably kept the weapons in case the conflict were again to break out (in the case of the arms caches, this is especially relevant). For some people, a weapon could have been a potential income generator; something to sell when times got tough. There were others who may have kept weapons to support future illegal activities, and still those people who were in fear of prosecution for declaring possession of an unlicensed arm (this may not have been the case immediately after the conflict, but certainly became a relevant reason later).'

Source: interview conducted April 2012.

final report were shared with the authorities and the general population. In surrounding countries, too, there were fears that remaining weapons could make their way across the borders. Subsequent reports indicate that these fears were later realised. According to Knight and Ozerdem (2004: 501), for example, the incomplete Mozambican disarmament process contributed 'to the proliferation of weapons, not only throughout that country, but also in neighbouring countries such as South Africa, Zambia and Malawi'. Moreover, 'by 1998, Mozambique constituted the single largest source of small arms to the South African domestic market' (*ibid*). Although this is a startling statement, the number of arms in circulation would have been significantly higher had it not been for certain initiatives within Mozambique which picked up where ONUMOZ left off.

FIC/FOMICRES

In Mozambique, as in many other countries, children were recruited by both sides in the conflict and fought as child soldiers. In 1995, a group of 14 Mozambican youths, which included a number of former child soldiers with combined experiences on the side of both the RENAMO and FRELIMO forces, came together at Massequessa, in the outskirts of Chimoio City in Manica Province to discuss effective ways for community participation in peacekeeping and security processes. They too worried that the disarmament process began by ONUMOZ remained incomplete and that failure to continue to collect and destroy the remaining weapons would endanger the peace process and national security. In the words of Albino Forquilha, the leader of the group:

'Many people were still traumatised by what had happened in the war and the devastated state of the country's economy, clinics and schools... We knew that with so many weapons in circulation, the fighting could be sparked again at any time' ('Different worlds same solutions', The Independent, May 2010).

With this in mind, the group established what they called an 'action of understanding', and adopted the name 'Community Intelligence Force' (Força de Inteligência Comunitária, or FIC).[8] The actions of FIC, initially at community level, were to:

1. Promote civic reconciliatory education among community members in order to build mutual trust.
2. Train community members on techniques to gain intelligence for public collection and destruction of small arms and light weapons that were still in illicit hands in the post-conflict period in Mozambique.

The group had substantial experience with both sides in the armed conflict, and had contacts that went deep inside the RE-NAMO camps, where many of the weapons caches were still held. As a result, FIC's members were in a strong position to elicit information from their contacts, without the informants fearing reprisals or worrying that their identity would be revealed to the authorities.

FIC initially had no legal organisational status, but was instead classified by the group itself as a patriotic movement. In addressing the disarmament issue, the group worked side by side with the Christian Council of Mozambique (CCM), which already had a wide network throughout the country, right down to the community

---

8 *For more information about FOMICRES, see: http://www.fomicres.org/index.html.*

level. FIC later established themselves as an NGO in their own right, becoming the organisation now known officially as the Mozambican Force for Crime Investigation and Social Reintegration (Força Moçambicana para Investigação de Crimes e Reinserção Social, or FOMICRES) in 2007. The disarmament project, jointly implemented by the members of FIC and the Christian Council of Mozambique, was called 'TAE' (Transformação de Armas em Enxadas), or 'turning arms into ploughshares'.[9]

TAE: arms into ploughshares

TAE's approach

The main objective of the TAE project was to foster a culture of peace and non-violence by encouraging people to participate in weapons collection and involve them in weapons destruction activities. The project comprised six components:

- Weapons collection.
- Exchange of weapons for tools.
- Destruction of weapons.
- Civic education in the community.
- Transformation of the destroyed weapons into art pieces.
- Post exchange follow-up with beneficiaries.

The transformation of weapons into art pieces was key to publicising the project. In many ways, this aspect has been the most visible internationally. However, given that this was only one component of the project (which has received considerable attention), this analysis instead focuses more on the first three components mentioned above,[10] in which members of FIC were most active.[11]

The weapons collection was heavily linked to the civic education aspect of the project. CCM was very well positioned to go into the communities and discuss the peacebuilding process and persuade

9 *The Portuguese name for the project was Transformação de Armas em Enxadas, which directly translated is 'turning arms into hoes'. However, it is also known in English 'Arms into Tools' or 'Transforming Arms into Ploughshares'.*

10 *For an analysis of the weapons into art component, see: Frank James Tester (2006). 'Art and Disarmament: Turning Arms into Ploughshares in Mozambique', Development in Practice, 16:02, 169-178.*

11 *During interviews, FOMICRES was often mentioned as the organisation that carried out the weapons collection, not CCM or TAE.*

Weapons search in family home

'One good example of how some weapons are hidden and controlled is the one we had in the area of Dombe in Manica Province where after considerable intelligence work with local collaborators, FOMICRES staff team discovered beneath a hut 125 very well conserved weapons (115 AKMs and 10 Pistols). Note that a complete family were living in this house, where under their beds were weapons. Interesting is that the mother (wife) and three kids were not aware of that because, according the holder of these weapons, this was a secret between him [former RENAMO Commandant] with his older child of 16 years.'

Source: FOMICRES Report, no date: 18.

---

people to come forward with weapons and/or information. However, CCM was not very knowledgeable in the area of weaponry itself, and thus it was here that FIC came in, with Albino Forquilha, the driving force behind FIC, becoming the project manager of this aspect of TAE activities.

In order to collect the weapons, first of all TAE had to discover where the weapons were, which was achieved in two ways. TAE personnel responsible for the weapons collection had a wealth of contacts with former combatants and leaders on both sides. These informants were often serving or demobilised soldiers from either the government forces or from RENAMO, many of whom were high-ranking officers. TAE personnel would use this network to discover the location of weapons, often operating via groups of volunteers and activists at district level, known as District Satellite Working Teams (DSWT), which would provide information to TAE headquarters in Maputo. Technical staff from Maputo would then travel to these areas to verify the information and subsequently collect the weapons and organise their destruction.

Staff and/or volunteers from TAE also travelled to districts where there were thought be to large amounts of weapons (based on knowledge, for example, of the areas that had been RENAMO strongholds). They would meet with the local authorities to explain the project and would then go on to directly inform the communities about their work. If an individual had information, he or she could discuss this in confidence with TAE personnel. Establishing

---

Building trust

Mr M lives in the countryside in Boane district, in the Province of Maputo. During the conflict in Mozambique, he was a high-ranking officer in the RENAMO forces. After the peace accord, he was one of those people integrated into the national defence forces. He currently lives with his family in a small house making his living from small-scale cultivation and raising some chickens and ducks. He is also now a church pastor.

During the conflict he was head of information for RENAMO, and thus had much information on where weapons were located. After the war, when the TAE project contacted him, he knew where the weapons were, and cooperated in informing the TAE contact. As a result, he received zinc sheeting, bicycles and a sewing machine. The zinc sheeting still covers the roof of his house, but some of the bicycles and the sewing machine are in disrepair and no longer being used.

Key to his readiness to cooperate with the project was the fact that the people who came to speak with him were also ex-military. In relation to the first contact made by the TAE operations officer, he said he trusted him because, 'He was military. I was military. I knew because of that he was not like others, who would sell me to the authorities.' It was important for him that the identity of the source was never revealed, and he never met directly with the police or other authorities, leaving this to TAE.

According to Mr M, many other people in the locality also received similar incentives for information and weapons, but he pointed out that despite the fact that some weapons remain, the work [of collection] had stopped because the funds for the incentives ran out.

Source: Interview with informant in Boane, conducted April 2012.

---

trust with local communities and beneficiaries took time and the TAE staff had to approach people with great care on this sensitive issue. As a former TAE operations officer says, 'The crucial part is the first interaction, first step. It must be done softly, slowly.'[12]

This provision of information was based on the idea that

---

12 Interview with former TAE/FOMICRES operations officer, conducted April 2012.

A duty to cooperate

Mr S was an informant/beneficiary of the TAE project. He lives in Boane in a small house that still has the zinc sheeting he received through the TAE project. He too had fought with RENAMO and had information about where ordnance material was after the conflict. He says when he and others in the community heard about the project, it took some time to establish trust, but the TAE people gave civic education talks, and spent much time with the people to establish trust.

As a result of information provided by himself and others in the community, they received zinc sheeting, ploughs, and bicycles. He says people agreed to give up the information and the arms because they felt it was their 'duty'. Of course, he adds, the incentives also helped, and even people who were initially reluctant, cooperated once they saw others receiving the incentives. Now, because they know there are no funds, people from Boane have stopped giving information.

He mentions that after the incentives stopped from the project, people still came to him sometimes with ordnance, and he would inform the district government, which initially gave incentives too, but then suddenly stopped, so they no longer trust the district government, as they had promised incentives but had not delivered them.

Source: Interview with informant in Boane, conducted April 2012.

informants, collaborators and beneficiaries would receive tools in return for weapons they surrendered. The tools included bicycles, sewing machines, sheets of zinc for roofing, agricultural tools and building materials. The type and number of tools received depended on the type and condition of the weapons handed over. TAE personnel would negotiate this on a case-by-case basis with the informant, but some general criteria were followed; for example, for 1 operational weapon (or 12 non-operational arms or 520 units of ammunition), an informant could expect to receive 10 zinc sheets or 1 bicycle.[13]

---

13 *This exchange criteria was mentioned in interviews with beneficiaries in April 2012 and in the BICC Brief 29 report, where it is indicated that 1 arm = 12 non-operational arms = 520 units of ammunition (Faltas and Paes, 2004: 27).*

Based on the information they received, TAE technical personnel, which numbered between two and five people over the course of the project, some trained by the South African Police Service, carried out the physical collection of the weapons. The weapons were organised by type and calibre, and the personnel involved would take photos, and register the information on a form. Most often, the collection of weapons was carried out by the TAE project, but on some occasions, where there were difficulties in accessing a cache, for example, TAE would instead pass the information on to Operation Rachel, which was a separate weapons collection collaboration between the Mozambican and South African police. Some people involved in the TAE project mentioned that Operation Rachel had far superior logistical means at its disposal, including helicopters to access difficult-to-reach locations.

The destruction process of the weapons and ordnance would subsequently be carried out either by TAE, in collaboration with the police or army, or directly by Operation Rachel personnel. Representatives from the community also attended to witness the process on behalf of the community. Media and donors were sometimes invited to view the destruction process.

Impact

Examining the impact of the TAE project is not straightforward. For example, the stated aim of the project was to support the creation of a culture of peace. However, when highlighting the success of the project, emphasis is usually placed on the number of weapons and other artefacts of war that were collected, which is then pointed to as an indicator of success. This is not to say that the collection of weapons and other ordnance is not linked to the culture of peace; nor is it to say that the artefacts of war collection work was not an extremely valuable project in the aftermath of the conflict. According to FOMICRES, community participation in the weapons collection was not solely based on the incentive system, but on a sense of wanting to participate in peacebuilding after the war. FOMICRES reports that there were communities who handed over weapons without demanding anything in return for their participation.[14]

---

14 *Email correspondence from Albino Forquilha, August 2012.*

It is interesting to note that in the case of the beneficiaries interviewed for this case study, the willingness to give up weapons and ordnance seemed to be more closely linked to the receipt of incentives than to a desire to promote peace and security. This is evidenced by the accounts of the two informants in Boane and also supported by the statements of others involved in the project. However, statements from FOMICRES indicate that whilst the role of incentives may have been a primary motivation for some communities, as in Boane, for example, the motivations for handing over weapons were in general based on a mixture of reasons.

Number of artefacts of war collected

If impact is examined in terms of weapons and other artefacts of war collected, as the TAE project has done, there are a few additional points to consider. It is important to mention that the amount of weapons collected by the TAE project has been reported incorrectly on occasion. One reason for this may have been errors in translation from Portuguese to English, or because of differences in classifications of 'weapons'. In various reports, including media reports made available by FOMICRES,[15] it is stated that over 800,000 weapons were collected. However, this cumulative figure actually refers to what in Portuguese is termed 'artefactos de guerra' (artefacts of war), and includes weapons, unexploded ordnance, and ammunition. The ONUMOZ report quotes a figure of 189,827 weapons collected, and it goes on to mention ammunition separately. However, in the ONUMOZ final report, it is unclear whether the weapons figure also includes items such as unexploded ordinance, landmines, etc. (Boutros-Ghali, 1994: 3). Reports that contrast the success of TAE versus ONUMOZ, at least in terms of weapons collected (ie, using the higher figure of 800,000 weapons), run the risk of somewhat reducing the credibility of the TAE project. Of course, this may not be the direct responsibility of the TAE project, given that these reports are primarily written by third parties.

Regardless of this issue about the reported number of weapons collected, the work completed by TAE is impressive for a civil society organisation. As the authors of the 2004 Bonn International

---

15 Sources: http://www.ssireview.org/articles/entry/competing_for_a_change/ and http://www.independent.co.uk/news/uk/home-news/independent-appeal-different-worlds-same-solutions-1857760.html.

Center for Conversion (BICC) report say:

> *'All things considered, for a church-run project to run a weapons collection program for seven years and collect thousands of guns and large quantities of ammunition and explosives is no mean achievement. For them to do this with very limited government support is remarkable'* (Faltas and Paes, 2004: 17).

With that in mind, some of the statistics in relation to the weapons collected are examined in the accompanying table.[16]

These figures indicate that the total number of weapons collected by TAE over the period 1995-2004 was 9,014, whilst the total figure for all ordnance (weapons, ammunition and so on) collected is 921,239. It must also be remembered that aside from the number of arms collected directly by TAE, the information that TAE provided to Operation Rachel also helped to uncover large quantities of arms and ammunition, particularly in regions that were logistically inaccessible to TAE personnel.

In fact, the collaboration between TAE and Operation Rachel was one of the strong points of the project. For the authorities, for example, TAE was able to get valuable information from the communities that Operation Rachel did not have access to. This collaboration continues until the present day, although now people speak of FOMICRES, and not TAE. As the National Focal Point for Small Arms in the Ministry of the Interior explains, 'In my opinion, they have the contacts, know people in the communities. If it's an area where we know there to be arms caches still, we ask FOMICRES to collaborate to gather information and collection.'[17]

Although TAE's original focus had been on individual owners of guns, information on arms caches in the country was gradually shared with TAE staff. According to FOMICRES' operations officer, as a result the organisation also began addressing this problem. In this aspect of TAE's work, the main challenge was the issue

---

16 *1995-2003 information is taken from the 2004 BICC assessment report, and confirmed by FOMICRES as accurate in April 2012; figures for 2003 onwards were compiled based on information received from FOMICRES in April 2012. Note that Zambezia and Cabo Delgado were two satellite offices operating semi-independently from the headquarters in Maputo.*

17 *Interview conducted April 2012.*

Table 1: Weapons collected by TAE 1995-2004

Type	1995	1996	1997	1998	1999	2000	2001	2002	Cabo Delgado (1995-2003) 2003	Cabo Delgado (1995-2003)	Zambezia (1995-2003)	Total 1995-2003	Cabo Delgado 2004 2003-2004	Cabo Delgado 2003-2004	Zambezia 2003-2004	Total
AKM	76	279	120	718	193	604	102	355	639	3	1582	4671	411	6	48	5136
Pistols	36	55	27	28	20	29	194	33	91	2	239	754	67	0	10	831
MG	2	7	1	6	5	5	1	0	0	0	14	41	3	0	3	47
PPX	82	79	85	17	84	13	6	69	120	1	5	561	99	0	1	661
Bazooka	17	14	5	53	12	3	0	0	31	0	15	150	27	0	7	184
Mortars	2	7	0	3	6	87	0	10	0	0	1	116	7	0	3	126
Machine Guns PK	1	9	3	18	1	3	0	0	0	0	42	77	2	2	11	92
Machine Guns Pieces	8	15	2	1	2	4	0	0	0	0	0	32	8	0	0	40
Mauser	12	23	4	2	9	15	9	12	0	0	197	283	82	1	9	375
G3	4	11	71	6	2	2	4	10	4	0	72	186	27	0	16	229
Semi-Automatics	19	10	145	13	13	5	19	1	4	0	34	263	210	0	5	478
Grenade Launchers	18	32	0	0	0	0	0	0	0	0	0	50	0	0	0	50
Rifles	3	1	2	2	1	7	221	1	52	1	229	520	6	0	42	568
FBP	0	0	0	0	0	0	0	80	29	0	0	109	49	0	0	158
M20	0	0	0	0	0	0	32	0	0	0	0	32	1	0	1	34
ZG1	0	1	0	0	0	0	2	0	0	0	2	5	0	0	0	5
Weapons collected	**280**	**543**	**465**	**867**	**348**	**777**	**590**	**571**	**970**	**7**	**2432**	**7850**	**999**	**9**	**156**	**9014**
Other items collected																
Explosives	1172	844	57	103	33	240	355	85	1856	34	1185	5964	905	4	772	7645
Ammunition	10489	9943	2881	33307	10226	19227	40059	22669	200507	3494	102907	455709	280771	118	166412	903010
Cartridges etc	147	128	371	187	26	112	160	46	3	0	8	1188	204	0	5	1397
Other equipment	5	7	1	0	2	4	1	3	6	0	1	30	8	3	9	50
Bayonets	75	4	1	1	0	34	0	0	3	0	2	120	0	0	3	123
Grand Total	**12168**	**11469**	**3776**	**34465**	**10635**	**20394**	**41165**	**23374**	**203345**	**3535**	**106535**	**470861**	**282887**	**134**	**167357**	**921239**

of transport, especially fuel costs[18] and storage of large quantities of weapons and other artefacts of war (see Leão, 2004b).

Impact on beneficiaries

The incentives received by beneficiaries are also important to consider when discussing impact. The general idea behind distributing tools instead of, for example, cash, was to give beneficiaries materials to allow them to start rebuilding their lives by engaging in business, cultivating land, reconstructing their homes and so on. Over the course of the project, it is estimated that up to 77,000[19] families received support in this way. Given the high number of ex-soldiers who found themselves jobless after the war, this support must have been very welcome, although the specific impact of this support has not been measured. Some comments from the BICC assessment suggest that although the incentives might not have directly benefitted poorer members of society, they may instead have benefitted indirectly. For example, the report cites an instance of a beneficiary who expanded his tailor shop as a result of receiving sewing machines from the project, which served to benefit the additional employees he had to hire. In general, the incentives were practical and aimed at assuring some longer-term benefits to beneficiaries and the broader communities in which they lived.[20]

Additional benefits related to the civic education aspect of the work. According to a FOMICRES report, 'space was opened for debates freely between government and civil society on the matter of security without fear and the criminality decreased.'[21] Although there is little evidence to directly support the claim of decreased criminality (statistics are unavailable or unreliable), it is certain that the work of TAE laid the groundwork for civil society participation in national security affairs, which is both unusual and positive. FOMICRES, CCM and other civil society organisations are now members of COPRECAL (Comissão Interministerial para Prevenção, Combate e Erradicação do Tráfico Ilícito de Armas Ligeiras e de Pequeno Porte), the national commission for small arms.

---

18 *Email correspondence from Albino Forquilha, August 2012.*
19 *Source: http://proxied.changemakers.net/journal/peace/displaypeace.cfm-ID=69.*
20 *Interview with Albino Forquilha, conducted April 2012.*
21 *Source: www.changemakers.com/competition/entrepreneuring-peace/entries/weapons-collection-community-based-peace-building-post.*

COPRECAL

This national commission has the authority to coordinate all small arms and light weapons control activities in the framework of the UNPOA.* COPRECAL was created in 2001 and promulgated by the Council of Ministers on 17 May 2005. The national commission has two levels: ministerial and technical. The ministerial level, which is political, is chaired by the Minister of the Interior, with the Minister of Defence acting as deputy chairperson. COPRECAL also has active representation from various ministers and is the main decision-making body. The technical level is the executive body and is chaired by the Permanent Secretary of the Ministry of Interior, comprising experts of the relevant ministries and civil society.

Roles and functions of COPRECAL:
1. Responsible for the coordination and integration of national efforts required to prevent, combat the illicit manufacturing, trade and use of small arms and light weapons.
2. Responsible for development and implementation of the National Action Plan to prevent, combat and eradicate the illicit manufacturing, trade, trafficking and use of small arms and light weapons (SALW).
3. Responsible for the implementation of the Southern African Development Community (SADC) Protocol on the Control of Firearms, Ammunition and Other Related Materials. It is also responsible for implementing other protocols, action plans and declarations pertaining to SALW, such as the United Nations Protocol, the UN POA, the Bamako Declaration and the Geneva Declaration on Armed Violence and Development.
4. Facilitating the exchange and dissemination of information pertaining to SALW.
5. Establishing and maintaining a national electronic database on SALW.
6. Coordinating and interacting with civil society and developing national public awareness programmes in the framework of the promotion of the culture of peace and nonviolence.

* UN Programme of Action on Small Arms and Light Weapons. See: http://www.poa-iss.org/.

Partnerships

The TAE project was based on several different types of partnerships and partners. For example, as already mentioned, the TAE project involved a group of civil society organisations, including collaboration between FIC (later known as FOMICRES) and CCM, with FIC personnel having the technical skills and the ex-military contacts that were vital to the success of the project. In turn, CMM had strong links at the grassroots community level that were valuable for TAE's educational components. TAE also forged strong relationships with security services in Mozambique and South Africa, especially under the auspices of Operation Rachel. The project also laid the groundwork for building links between government and civil society.

For example, some of the technical staff working on the TAE project received training from the South African Police Service (SAPS) in 1995. This was around the time that the South African and Mozambican police were beginning their collaboration under Operation Rachel. Lacking informants on the ground, SAPS trained a number of ex-soldiers from Mozambique to support them in the process of gathering intelligence on arms caches, with some of these trainees acting in support of both Operation Rachel and TAE. Where TAE was logistically unable to collect an arms cache, they shared that information with Operation Rachel, which would then collect the weapons. Operation Rachel also oversaw destruction of ordnance collected by TAE.

Although Operation Rachel had superior logistical means, it was understood that the TAE project was complementary to Operation Rachel. In the words of an official from the Ministry of the Interior (Ministério do Interior, or MINT), the advantage of the TAE project was clear: 'When MINT, or police, or armed forces appear, the message is not always accepted by the community. The impact is better when it's civil society. People are nervous, afraid of authorities sometimes.'[22]

In 1995 when TAE began collecting weapons, Mozambique was the first country in the world where the government had given this responsibility to a civil society organisation (Faltas and Paes, 2004:

---

22 *Interview with national focal point for small arms, Ministry of the Interior, conducted April 2012.*

Operation Rachel

'From the mid-1990s incidents of crime involving firearms in both South Africa and Mozambique noticeably increased. According to intelligence reports by the South African police, a substantial number of the firearms used to commit crime in South Africa had originated from weapons caches in Mozambique. Consequently in 1995, the governments of Mozambique and South Africa established Operation Rachel, with the objective of destroying arms caches in Mozambique.

Operation Rachel has consisted of a number of phases in which teams of Mozambican and South African police personnel have travelled throughout Mozambique identifying and destroying arms caches. During the eight operations between 1995 and 2003, over 600 arms caches were discovered and several tons of arms and ammunition were destroyed. Prior to the Rachel operations, the price of an AK-47 in Soweto was around R100; in 2003, the same weapon cost 3000 Rand indicating the decrease in firearm availability in South Africa since the beginning of the operation.'

Source: Leão (2004a: 109-100)

---

9).[23] The fact that TAE operated independently from government was an advantage in that it was easier to gain the trust of communities, and thereby to access information.

However, some reports (eg, the BICC report from 2004) speculate that this independence was a negative factor since it meant that TAE did not have full access to government, military and police expertise. In fact, this does not seem to be entirely fair, as there was clear collaboration between TAE and Operation Rachel. Presumably, this cooperation could have been greater, but there was always the risk that too close a connection with official authorities would have given TAE less leverage in the communities.

One caution that is raised in the BICC report is that the TAE project did not serve to increase public confidence in the ability of government to maintain security. Whilst there may be some validity in this statement, the other side of the argument is that the project highlighted the role that civil society can play in national security

---

23 *Also confirmed by Albino Forquilha in interview conducted April 2012.*

matters. Presently, at the level of the Ministry of the Interior, it is clear that much importance is attached to this role, and various mentions are made of the excellent relationships which civil society and government have, through both previous collaborations and now formally through the COPRECAL structure.[24] In fact, the civil society presence in COPRECAL is so strong that FOMICRES itself has represented the commission in international meetings in recent years.

Donors

Funders of the TAE project have been many. The initiative captured the imagination of donors; some quite likely as a result of the visible weapons-into-art component, in which Mozambican artists created sculptures from the destroyed weapons. These sculptures went on to be displayed worldwide, and drew attention to the efforts in Mozambique.

The 2004 BICC report mentions support from Press Alternative and the Mozambique Development Corporation Japan Committee, both from Japan, Arche Nova from Germany, Cuso International and the Canadian International Development Agency (CIDA) from Canada, plus organisations from the Netherlands, South Africa, Sweden and the US.

In this and in other reports[25] about the TAE project, the governments of Norway and Switzerland are mentioned, as well as UN agencies. In addition to funds received, there was support in kind received from Japan in the form of 12 containers of bicycles that were used as incentives (see Vallely, 2010).

Effectiveness

Evaluation

Two major assessments/evaluations of the TAE project were carried out. One was commissioned by World Vision Germany and carried out by the Bonn International Center for Conversion (BICC) in

---

24 *Interview with national focal point for small arms, Ministry of the Interior, conducted April 2012.*
25 *Source: http://proxied.changemakers.net/journal/peace/displaypeace.cfm-ID=69.*

2004.[26] Another assessment/study was undertaken by the Canadian NGO CUSO and the Canadian International Development Agency (CIDA) in 2006.[27] The second study concentrates more on the weapons-into-art component of the project, whilst the first focuses very much on the weapons collection aspect. Here the focus is on the first evaluation.

At the outset, it is necessary to mention that those involved with the TAE project did not fully accept the results of the report produced by BICC. In fact, the report was not officially recognised and endorsed by the TAE project because there were a number of points of disagreement in relation to the report that were never resolved to the satisfaction of TAE.

At the same time, however, the BICC report does contain much information that is valid in terms of analysis of the work of TAE. Whilst critical, the report highlighted a number of positive lessons learned:

> 'One can go on to admire the way TAE has put the issue of illegal guns on the map in Mozambique, widely promoted the idea of replacing them by something peaceful and useful, and actually carried out thousands of such exchanges. Besides, one can point out that this is a unique example of civil society taking the job of weapons reduction into its own hands, even if in reality the government provides more support to TAE than meets the eye. Surely, one might argue, this is a shining example for other poor countries with weak governments to follow' (Faltas and Paes, 2004: 33).

The BICC reported concluded that whilst there is much to be learned from the TAE project, certain specific points should be taken into account before it is replicated in any other countries. Some of these relate to:

- **The motivation of gun holders.** Understanding not only who has weapons, but also the purpose for which they are retaining them is key in devising a strategy of voluntary weapons return. Offering material incentives can be useful, but civic

---

26 For a full copy of BICC Brief 29 by Faltas and Paes, see: http://www.bicc.de/uploads/tx_bicctools/brief29.pdf.
27 See: Frank James Tester (2006). 'Art and disarmament: turning arms into ploughshares in Mozambique', Development in Practice, 16:02, 169-178.

education and awareness-raising on the potential dangers of the firearms themselves is important, especially for individuals retaining weapons for self-protection. Work also needs to be done to convince people of the capacity of the police to offer adequate protection from danger.

- **Project aims.** The stated aim of the project was to foster a culture of peace, and the BICC report concludes that this was indeed achieved: 'The mere act of surrendering and destroying weapons can, if well publicized, contribute enormously to a peace process by increasing trust among the population. This is particularly true when programs make a deliberate effort not to target a specific group or geographical area, but encompass participants from all sides and therefore take a non-partisan stand' (Faltas and Paes, 2004: 34).

  However, as has been done in some reports, measuring the success of the project based on the number of arms collected is problematic, since the number of weapons was actually quite small in comparison to the estimates for weapons present in the country.

- **Provision of incentives.** The incentives approach can be very useful, but may be more useful where the black market for weapons is small, and/or demand is low. Additionally, whilst physical donations of incentives from distant overseas countries can appear to be cost-effective, there can be hidden costs associated with this (shipping, customs and handling fees), and this should be weighed against procuring the same goods locally using cash donations received. This can also factor into overall local economic development.

In addition to these points, the BICC evaluation report highlights the need for focused training on safe handling and storage of weapons for any individual or organisation involved in weapons collection. Likewise, adequate equipment and resources are required. Furthermore, it is necessary that there is a body adequately trained and equipped to carry out the destruction/ decommissioning process. This could be a government body, or a sub-contractor, for example.

Cost effectiveness: comparison with other initiatives

Although some reports mentioning the project refer to its cost effectiveness,[28] it is difficult to make direct cost comparisons between the various initiatives. This is due, for example, to the different nature and scope of the interventions, differences in the duration of the interventions and the lack of information on the breakdown of costs and activities.

It is reported, for example, that the ONUMOZ mission spent a total of US$113 million on its DDR component, whereas the TAE project cost US$6 million.[29] The cost of Operation Rachel (1995-2001) is estimated at US$1.3 million.[30] At first glance, it may look like Operation Rachel was the most cost effective (over 19,000 weapons collected, compared with 189,000 and 9,000 for ONUMOZ and TAE, respectively). However, such a comparison does not take into account various factors, some of which are:

- Comparing cost effectiveness based on weapons collected and costs of each initiative would seem to make the assumption is that all three initiatives classify 'weapons' similarly. Whilst this appears to be the case for TAE and Operation Rachel, ONUMOZ figures may also include items such as tanks, armoured personnel carriers and mines (but not ammunition).
- The cost in relation to the ONUMOZ mission was the amount for 'demobilising, reinserting and reintegrating 92,881 former combatants', and not only the cost of the actual weapons collection. Similarly, the TAE project conducted awareness raising activities, and not only weapons collection.
- It must be remembered that work completed by TAE (and therefore costs incurred by the project) led to some of the weapons that were discovered being collected by Operation Rachel. This refers both to information and weapons handed over for destruction to Operation Rachel. It is not clear how many of the weapons collected under Operation Rachel were due to support from TAE, or if there is any double reporting.
- It is also not clear whether the costs of Operation Rachel include costs of the personnel (either South African or Mozambican police). Thus the real cost of Operation Rachel may in fact be higher than the US$1.3 million mentioned above.

---

28 *In particular, this is a point made in Ripples into Waves (Peace Direct, 2010). See: http://www.insightonconflict.org/from-local-to-national-peacebuilding/.*
29 *Ibid, 4.*
30 *Source: http://www.iss.co.za/Pubs/Papers/53/Paper53.htm.*

Assertions that the TAE project represented an extremely cost-effective method of weapons collection are thus impossible to confirm or refute, given the lack of crucial background information and concrete evidence that could offer a basis for comparative evaluation. This is worth noting for future projects that wish to analyse cost effectiveness in an in-depth manner.

The role of incentives

The approach TAE took in the use of incentives was to distribute items that provided material benefits in the short and medium term. As mentioned before, this included zinc sheeting, bicycles, sewing machines, farming tools, and items such as seeds. In contrast to a cash incentive programme, this approach was a very positive aspect of the TAE project. In particular, it minimised the problems seen elsewhere with cash incentives being used in less productive ways. For example, it was reported in Liberia that cash incentives were used for 'alcohol, drugs and sex workers'.[31]

The incentives provided by the TAE project went some way toward allowing recipients to rebuild their lives and to engage in productive activities. However, the provision of these incentives alone may not be sufficient. The most effective approach is a comprehensive programme that offers opportunities for 'new, non-violent livelihoods' (Knight and Ozerdem, 2004: 505).

Conclusions and recommendations

The TAE project was clearly effective as a complementary initiative to Operation Rachel, and served its role in promoting peace in the country after the conflict. The ceremonies where weapons were destroyed were vital components in making people feel safe once again. As a result of TAE's work (and subsequently the work of FOMICRES), the place of civil society in the control of small arms and light weapons, and in promoting human security, is well recognised by the Government of Mozambique and by donors. In recent years, FOMICRES, comprised of the technical staff component from the TAE project, has shifted priorities from the collection

---

31 Sources: *http://www.irinnews.org/Report/93354/Analysis-How-best-to-remove-guns -from-post-conflict-zones.*

and destruction of artefacts of war to cooperation with the government, in particular in the area of community safety and security. This would seem to make sense for a country that has made the successful transition from conflict to peace. It also responds to the perceived needs of communities in Mozambique.

The project offers useful lessons to other organisations engaged in or planning a similar model in other countries. Some of these lessons have already been outlined above. Nonetheless, it is useful to summarise those here, as well as mention additional points:

1. Projects should be clear on their focus, and on how the impact of the project will be measured. In TAE's case, the aim was to create peace through community involvement in weapons collection and destruction. However, on occasion, the focus on displaying impact by highlighting how many artefacts of war were collected presents a disconnect from the main objective.

2. Any organisation conducting weapons collection should have:
   - Legal mandates to do so.
   - Adequate training on the safe handling of ordnance, etc.
   - Adequate resources for collection and storage of the ordnance.

3. Incentives can and do work, and provide opportunities for employment and livelihoods in a post-conflict period, but care should be taken that other methods are also employed to persuade people to part with weapons. The TAE project did this through awareness raising and educational activities. Without this, there is the risk that once the incentive runs out, people no longer cooperate. A 'carrot and stick' approach may be appropriate, with an amnesty and incentives during the collection period, and penalties for arms not given up by the end of the collection period.

4. In addition to weapons collection, organisations should ensure that community education and awareness raising activities teach people the danger of weapons, appropriate handling of arms, etc.

5. Civil society organisations, especially those that have contacts on both sides of the conflict (most notably military, paramilitary and rebel militia contacts), offer a unique advantage in getting information about individual weapons and other arte-

facts of war retained after conflict, as well as larger caches of weapons and related war materials.

6. Cooperation/collaboration between civil society and police/army-led initiatives is essential, but a certain distance needs to be maintained in order not to appear 'on the side' of government, at least until trust has been established between communities and the authorities. This process of building trust will undoubtedly take time, and programmes that aim for long-term peacebuilding should factor this into their plans.

7. Initiatives such as weapons-into-art can be useful to attract international attention and funds. They can also have value in the local context in that they visually represent the reconciliation and/or commemoration process.

8. Cooperation with government is essential, and governments should endeavour to support civil society work in peacebuilding. Governments should try to create a space for civil society in national commissions (for small arms) and where appropriate, the government needs to create legal conditions for a civil society actor to carry out weapons collection. In addition, amnesties need to be provided during collection periods, whilst penalties for holding weapons after the end of the collection period should be clearly outlined and enforced.

9. Gender aspects of weapons collection projects need to be considered. In this case, most of the beneficiaries were men, although women are equally or more impacted by the negative effects of arms/armed violence.

10. In recording information on weapons and artefacts of war that have been collected, organisations should be:
   • Clear in categorising types of weapons and ordnance.
   • Transparent in reporting these figures to the general public, donors and the media.

References

Berman, Eric. *Managing Arms in Peace Processes: Mozambique.* Geneva: UNIDIR, 1999.

FOMICRES Report. 'Small Arms Survey Additional Information'. Unpublished, no date.

Leão, Ana. 'Country Report: Mozambique' in Hide and Seek: Taking Account of Small Arms in Southern Africa. Eds. Chandré Gould and Guy Lamb. Pretoria: Institute for Security Studies, October 2004(a).

Leão, Ana. Monograph 94: Weapons in Mozambique, Reducing Availability and Demand. Pretoria: Institute for Security Studies, January 2004(b).

Morgan, Glenda. 'Violence in Mozambique: Towards an Understanding of RENAMO', Journal of Modern African Studies, Vol. 28, No. 4 (1990).

Murdock, Janet and Alfiado Zunguza. The Cumulative Impacts of Peacebuilding in Mozambique. Cumulative Impact Case Study. Reflecting on Peace Practice Project. Cambridge, MA: CDA Collaborative Learning Projects, April 2010.

Smith, Christopher. 'The International Trade in Small Arms', Jane's Intelligence Review, Vol. 7, No. 9 (1995), pages 427-430 in Eric Berman, Managing Arms in Peace Processes: Mozambique. Geneva: UNIDIR, 1999.

Faltas, Sami and Wolf-Christian Paes. Exchanging Guns for Tools. The TAE Approach to Practical Disarmament – an Assessment of the TAE Project in Mozambique. BICC Brief 29. Bonn: Bonn International Center for Conversion, 2004.

Boutros-Ghali, Boutros (ONUMOZ final report). Final Report of the Secretary-General on the United Nations Operation in Mozambique. New York: UN Security Council, December 1994.

Knight, Mark and Alpaslan Ozerdem. 'Guns, Camps and Cash: Disarmament, Demobilization and Reinsertion of Former Combatants in Transitions from War to Peace', Journal of Peace Research, Vol. 41, No. 4, 2004, pages 499-516.

Vallely, Paul. 'Independent Appeal: Different Worlds, Same Solutions. A Former Child Soldier is Showing Londoners How to Overcome Conflict', The Independent, 5 January 2010.

Building justice from the grassroots in Cambodia: IBJ

by Nastasia Bach, Kate Flower and Jessica Knowles [1]

The narrative of Local First now moves on to the theme of good governance, with this fourth case study on International Bridges to Justice (IBJ) in Cambodia. This collection also changes geographical direction. IBJ Cambodia is a compelling example of a locally owned approach. After the Khmer Rouge destroyed the country's legal system, Legal Aid Cambodia, a local NGO, invited Geneva-based IBJ to join its efforts to provide legal assistance to the poor and encourage the government to undertake judicial reform. This reveals a key insight about Local First: the importance of building existing local capacities wherever they are found. Here, IBJ Cambodia takes a multiple approach to local needs – for more and better trained defenders, and for greater competence across the entire judicial sector, including the courts and prison service. Crucially, it also meets a need for broader legal empowerment, educating citizens about their legal rights, while also establishing an MoU with the Government of Cambodia to create a sustainable state-operated legal aid system.

'I remember peering through the bars of a cell in Cambodia and talking with a young boy who had been detained, tortured by the police, and was languishing in prison, confused and daunted by what would or could happen next. Like most prisoners in Cambodia, he had no lawyer or human rights worker to defend him or safeguard his rights, and he had no pending trial date to determine his guilt or innocence. I flashed back to ten years before, to my college days of organizing letter-writing campaigns for political prisoners. We had demanded that they be free from torture and be granted their right to fair and speedy trials. But as I came face to face with this young boy, I realized that neither I nor my fellow students would have

---

1 *Among other sources, this case study is based on internal IBJ Cambodia documents and a range of interviews conducted by the authors with relevant justice sector stakeholders throughout Cambodia in 2012. The authors wish to gratefully acknowledge their coopera-tion. They also wish to thank Brian Rohan, Special Projects Director at IBJ headquarters in Geneva, for his significant contribution to this text.*

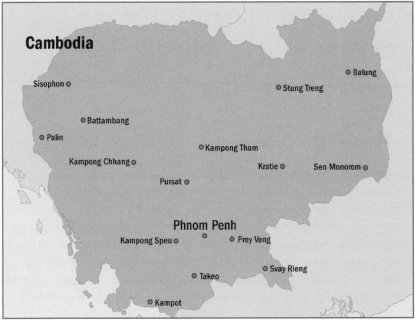

Map showing impact of project

written a letter for him. He was not a political prisoner; he was just an unimportant 12 year old boy whose mischievous behavior, trying to steal a bicycle, had landed him in this quandary' – Karen Tse, IBJ's Founder and CEO.

Post-conflict Cambodia: background context

The Kingdom of Cambodia is home to nearly 15 million people, spread across 23 provinces and one municipality. Over one third of the population lives below the national poverty line (Government of Australia, 2007: 3), and the country ranks 139 out of 187 countries on the Human Development Index.[2] A former French colony, Cambodia's legal system was based on the French system following independence in 1953 until the rise of the Khmer Rouge in 1975.

Under the Khmer Rouge, all government and social service institutions were abolished and systematic killings targeted

---

2 UNDP, *Human Development Index Rankings, 2011*. See: *http://www.undp. org/content/dam/undp/library/corporate/HDR/2011%20Global%20HDR/English/ HDR_2011_EN_Complete.pdf.*

dissidents, intellectuals and professionals, including lawyers and judges. The party exercised supreme power as judge and executioner, and an estimated 1.7 million people – 21 per cent of the population – lost their lives from 1975 to 1979.[3] Not including the refugees who fled, only an estimated six to ten lawyers and judges survived the Khmer Rouge genocide in Cambodia (Hor et al, 2012: 484).

The Vietnamese military invaded Cambodia in 1979, and during the protracted civil war that followed, the legal system was strongly influenced by the Vietnamese model, which is a combination of communist legal theory and French civil law. In 1991, decades of conflict ended with the signing of the Paris Peace Agreement and the subsequent UN peacekeeping operation. In 1993, a new constitution was adopted that endorsed international standards of human rights. In 1994, Cambodia had just begun to emerge from an extremely dark period of genocide and civil war. The extended conflict had dismantled most government institutions, including the justice system, which has had to be rebuilt from scratch.

In the two decades since then, the Cambodian legal system has been defined by its Khmer, French, and common law influences. The current judicial system includes a Supreme Court, an Appellate Court, provincial courts, a military court, and the Extraordinary Chambers in the Courts of Cambodia – established to prosecute senior leaders of the Khmer Rouge for crimes against humanity.

As a result of all of this upheaval, the modern Cambodian legal system faces many obstacles in providing access to justice for all citizens. The lack of basic infrastructure, including educational opportunities, qualified professionals, and adequate funding and resources, thwarts the functioning of the justice system (Hammarberg, 1997: 3).[4] The lack of specialised training is especially dire: in 2000, out of 171 Cambodian judges, 40 per cent had only secondary school education, and 7 per cent had attended only primary school. Additionally, just 9 per cent of prosecutors had earned a legal degree (UN, 2009: 78).

This situation is now changing, with training programmes for judges and prosecutors now in place. Yet, substantive trainings are

---

3 See: Cambodian Genocide Program, Yale University, http://www.yale.edu/cgp/.
4 Thomas Hammarberg was the Special Representative of the Secretary General for Human Rights in Cambodia from 1996 to 2000.

only part of the issue. Further compounding the insufficiencies of the justice system, legal decisions are often strongly influenced by corruption as well as political pressure (*ibid*, 87). Public servants, including police, lawyers, clerks, and judges, are rarely paid a living wage and thus often supplement their income through bribes (Government of Australia, 2007: 2). Cases move through the justice system at a rate proportional to the bribes paid to court officials or due to the political sensitivity of the case (Un, 2009: 76). As a result, indigent defendants suffer while the wealthy or politically influential commit crimes with impunity.

The Cambodian detention and prison systems are similarly lacking in basic infrastructure and resources, and as a result often violate detainees' and prisoners' human rights. Due to budget constraints, food rations are insufficient (Hammarberg, 1997: 4), and the sluggish justice system contributes to massive overcrowding. As the criminal justice system began to rebuild, the prison population quickly expanded.[5] Between 1998 and 2003, for example, the prison population nearly doubled, and all prisons had either reached capacity or were over-capacity (LICADHO, 2004: 15). Since then, the prison population has grown at a rate of 14 per cent per year, placing the prison system, which now has a total of 27 prisons, at 167 per cent capacity (LICADHO, 2010: 1). Overcrowding contributes to the spread of disease and places severe strains on already scarce resources such as food, clean water, sanitation systems, and medicine.

In addition to overcrowded and unsanitary living conditions, detainees and prisoners are also vulnerable to torture at the hands of police, prison guards, and other prisoners. The police forces' utilisation of torture to extract confessions during interrogations was so widespread in 1997 that it drew the attention of the Special Representative of the Secretary General for Human Rights for the United Nations (Hammarberg, 1997: 4). Although overall rates of torture of detainees and prisoners declined from 1999 to 2006, reported rates of torture of detainees in police custody increased from 2004 to 2006 (LICADHO, 2007: 18).

---

5 *This period marks the start of rebuilding Cambodian judicial institutions, including the prison system. Growing external pressures to implement rule of law, combined with lengthy pre-trial detention, are usually given as the explanation for the increase in the number of prisoners during this time (Hammarberg, 1997: 4).*

IBJ defender profile: Khmer Rouge survivor and former police officer Ouk Vandeth

IBJ's Cambodia Country Manager Ouk Vandeth was a 20-year-old student at a Buddhist monastery when the Khmer Rouge came to power. He was forced to work as a farmer at a labour camp.

Vandeth met his wife while working in the labor camps. When the Khmer Rouge regime collapsed in 1979 they fled to the border, where Vandeth became a soldier against the Vietnamese invasion. In 1985 he was made the deputy police officer of a refugee camp for displaced Cambodians and witnessed many human rights violations by his fellow police officers. 'In my duty, I found many mistakes,' he says. 'My colleagues got the confession from the accused – but by torture, threat or by cheat... I thought: we are violating the rights of the people and we cannot find justice.'

Strongly affected by the torture he had witnessed, Vandeth decided to become a defence attorney. He was trained by IBJ founder Karen Tse in the early 1990s and became one of Cambodia's first public defenders. 'These experiences made me become a defender,' he says. 'It was my mistake, the mistake of my society. I need to change the minds of the people – what is justice?'

In 1996, Ouk Vandeth was named head of the Kandal provincial office of Legal Aid of Cambodia, a newly created NGO providing broad legal assistance to the poor. Yet from his first-hand experience, he realised that of all the legal problems facing poor and vulnerable Cambodians, the gravest situation of all was that faced by the indigent accused. Dedicating himself to promoting the rights of the accused, Vandeth joined IBJ in 2007 to open the first office in Cambodia.

When he reflects on what IBJ has accomplished in just four short years, there are many changes to be proud of: 'When there is an IBJ defender, there is no corruption,' he says. 'The police have now started to stop the torture and they now receive training on skills to investigate... and the police themselves are afraid about being found guilty of torture because torture is now a crime.'

Source: interview conducted 5 June 2012.

IBJ Cambodia's Defender Resource Center model

Vandeth and Karen have been working together to strengthen the Cambodian justice sector for over a decade. In 2001, Legal Aid of Cambodia (LAC), a local legal assistance non-governmental organisation (NGO), first invited IBJ to join its efforts to provide legal assistance to the poor. After witnessing the direct and immediate impact that access to a lawyer had in the provinces of Cambodia, Vandeth and Karen decided in 2007 to undertake a focused effort specifically defending the rights of the accused.

In February of 2008, IBJ opened its first offices in Phnom Penh, Cambodia. Following a three-month baseline survey, IBJ Cambodia realised that there was extremely limited legal assistance available in the provinces. After securing funding from EuropeAID and WISE, IBJ Cambodia began a three year programme to bring legal aid to the provinces, opening offices in Takeo and Pursat provinces. A year later, IBJ Cambodia received further funding from East West Management Institute to open an office in Prey Veng, and in 2010 opened two more offices in the provinces of Mondulkiri and Rattanakiri. In 2012, IBJ Cambodia further expanded its reach and opened an additional three offices in Battambang, Banteay Meanchey and Kampong Thom provinces through the support of Australian Aid for International Development (AusAID).[6]

IBJ Cambodia now has 31 local staff working towards strengthening the criminal justice system. Each provincial office is staffed with a lawyer, an investigator and an administrative assistant and operates what IBJ calls a Defender Resource Center (DRC). The DRCs provide permanent legal aid in their respective provinces, as well as legal aid assistance in one other neighbouring province. Each DRC works to achieve three specific objectives:

- Provide high-quality legal aid services to Cambodians who would otherwise be denied access to a lawyer, or would be provided a lawyer only at the last stage possible, which would lead to rights violations, unfair trials, excessive pre-trial detention and greater risk of torture as an investigative tool.
- Build capacity of both local and national level justice stake-

---

6 *In large part, this expansion was based on an IBJ Cambodia baseline survey conducted in March 2012 that recorded a 100 per cent conviction rate in Kampong Thom, a province severely under-served by public defenders, with lawyers only present at the trial stage.*

holders to interpret and implement the laws correctly. In order to do so, IBJ Cambodia has developed collaborative and trusting relationships with key justice sector stakeholders throughout Cambodia: the local authorities and national officials in the best position to ensure that the human rights of the accused are properly upheld, and the criminal defence lawyers whose role is to provide early and competent legal counsel to the accused.

- Empower ordinary Cambodian citizens and indigenous communities with the knowledge of their basic legal rights and empower them to exert their rights in the context of any interactions with the Cambodian justice system.

Working towards these objectives, IBJ Cambodia now operates eight DRCs in rural provinces and one national DRC in Phnom Penh. These DRCs also cover a neighbouring province, thus enabling IBJ Cambodia to provide services to a total of 17 out of 24 Cambodian provinces and municipalities. Through its nine offices throughout Cambodia, IBJ holds seminars and training sessions to help train lawyers and inform justice stakeholders and citizens of their rights. At these seminars and trainings, the law is disseminated, and the audience is given the opportunity to discuss problems specific to their work, social life and prevailing situations at the commune and province level.

The main function of the DRCs is to support local defenders by providing them with the training and resources they need to provide the highest possible quality of legal representation to persons accused of crimes in their local communities. They also engage in a constructive dialogue with various local justice sector stakeholders to promote the role of defenders in criminal justice, and conduct street law campaigns to increase awareness among the general population of the rights of the accused. IBJ staff further engage clients through court appointments, monthly prison visits and legal consultations, and work closely with other NGOs, especially community based organisations, in an effort to provide every Cambodian citizen with early access to competent legal representation.

'I have many reasons that motivate me to work for IBJ. The first is to provide pro bono defence to the poor. Without my defence, my clients would be given the maximum sentence, which in most cases is

unfair. If my clients are innocent, I aim to prove this and have them acquitted. IBJ has been increasingly recognised by competent authorities throughout Takeo and Kampot as well as by the local people. This awareness is due to our street law trainings and by word-of-mouth. I have direct contact with the police who can contact me by phone at any time. Having direct access to our clients held in police custody provides a real opportunity to prevent them from being tortured and guarantees their right to a fair trial. This is IBJ's mission and purpose' (Kin Vibol, IBJ Cambodia lawyer for Takeo Province, interview conducted 24 April 2012).

The DRCs also play a significant role in providing poor, indigenous and marginalised persons with access to legal services, legal representation and education.

IBJ's programmes build awareness, technical capacity and trust of justice stakeholders in Cambodia to form the building blocks for IBJ's long-term goal: a sustainable criminal justice system that guarantees all citizens the right to competent legal representation, the right to be protected from cruel and unusual punishment and the right to a fair trial.

Programme components: creating impact

The dream of a fair and impartial justice system that respects the dignity of all sets the tone for IBJ Cambodia's mission: to protect the basic legal rights of ordinary Cambodians by ensuring that everyone has the right to competent legal representation, protection from cruel and unusual punishment and the right to a fair trial. IBJ Cambodia achieves this through four specific components that comprise its overall work: providing early access to counsel; educating and changing justice stakeholders' attitudes about the role of the justice system; improving the skills of defenders; and empowering citizens with knowledge of their legal rights. The overarching vision from this holistic approach to change is to build the infrastructure to create a fair and sustainable justice system in Cambodia.

Increasing access to justice: Defender Resource Centers
To increase access to justice throughout Cambodia, IBJ Cambodia

Successes and challenges in the provinces: Kratie, Rattanakiri, and Kampong Thom

After a year of working in Kratie province, starting from an initially strained relationship and resistance from the local justice sector, IBJ Cambodia is now referred cases directly from the court. This means that accused persons have a lawyer before trial and IBJ Cambodia's investigator gathers evidence to establish the facts of the case. It means the right to a fair trial.

Another very significant achievement for IBJ Cambodia is in Rattanakiri province, one of the most isolated provinces in the entire country. The police themselves now regularly call IBJ Cambodia's lawyer to the police station after a person has been arrested. This is an enormous achievement with immediate and positive impact. In May 2012 alone, IBJ Cambodia's lawyer was able to obtain the release of two clients with all charges dropped, due to a lack of evidence, within 48 hours after arrest. Without this early intervention from a lawyer, the accused would have automatically been charged by the police and sent to prison to wait for months in an overcrowded prison, exposed to harsh and unsanitary conditions, diseases and the threat of torture.

In Kampong Thom province, the location of IBJ Cambodia's newest office, an evaluation of cases brought before the court during a one-month period prior to IBJ Cambodia's engagement in the province revealed that only in felony or juvenile cases was a lawyer even present; moreover, this lawyer only was appointed at the final stage of the process: the trial date. There was no investigation or evidence gathering by the lawyer whatsoever and 100 per cent of the cases ended in conviction. With a country-wide dismissal or acquittal rate of 20 per cent in those areas where it is active, it is clear that IBJ Cambodia is providing essential services to ordinary Cambodians and having a fundamental impact on the workings of justice.

encourages lawyers to shift their attention from Phnom Penh to the provinces. By having DRCs in the provinces, citizens throughout the country have reliable, early access to legal support. There are now legal aid services in a total of 17 of the 24 provinces and municipalities, which has created significant short and long-term impacts. In the short-term, IBJ Cambodia has provided legal aid representation to over 3,000 clients. The long-term impact of this legal aid representation, conducted in combination with the other programming components (such as justice sector roundtables and public awareness work), is the development of a more efficient justice system in the most remote corners of the country and better protection against torture, excessive pre-trial detention and other inhumane treatment or punishment.

'I used to have to ask the Cambodian Bar Association to send a lawyer, but sometimes the lawyers that they would send were unprepared or busy. We would have to postpone the trial. Now we have a chance to meet with the IBJ lawyer immediately and prepare together' (Muong Savin, Prey Veng Prosecutor, interview conducted 24 May 2012).

Changes in attitudes of justice stakeholders: trainings and roundtables

To improve the implementation of the law, IBJ Cambodia works towards changing the attitudes of justice stakeholders at both the national and local levels. In practical terms, this means engaging directly with justice stakeholders to train them about Cambodian law and correct methods of application.

Creating effective partnerships is essential for IBJ Cambodia's work. At the national level, IBJ Cambodia works with the Ministry of Justice to implement its legal aid work and conduct its education and training programmes. To solidify this partnership, the Ministry of Justice and IBJ Cambodia signed a Memorandum of Understanding (MoU) in May 2012, including the following agreements:

- Continue to increase and improve access to justice.
- Improve and promote human rights.
- Strengthen the rule of law.
- Encourage early access to a lawyer.
- Commit to citizen education of law and human rights.
- Ensure consistency in the application of the law by all justice stakeholders and law enforcement officers throughout Cambodia.

The MoU promotes cooperation between the Ministry of Justice and IBJ Cambodia to create a sustainable, state-operated legal aid system in Cambodia. As such, it is an important step towards building the foundation and structure for a strong and equitable criminal justice sector that is locally conceived and appropriate to the local context. The MoU itself is a tremendous achievement: such arrangements between NGOs and government are uncommon, particularly in the justice sector. However, after years of relationship building and collaboration, the Ministry now not only understands the tremendous value of IBJ Cambodia's approach, but with this MoU has now become a key proponent of it.

'I would like more transparency in the decision making of the courts and I would like all Cambodians to understand the law so that they can defend themselves' (His Excellency Ang Vong Vathna, Minister of Justice, interview conducted 5 April 2012).

At the local level, IBJ Cambodia provides training and legal dissemination sessions to judges, prosecutors, police and prison officials on the correct interpretation and implementation of the law. In particular, IBJ Cambodia trains justice stakeholders on the new Criminal Procedure Code and Criminal Code that were enacted in 2010. Training is approached in two different ways:

1. In partnership with the Under-Secretary of State of the Ministry of Justice, IBJ Cambodia has held a number of three-day training events for the judicial police, military police and prison officials. These training sessions emphasise the illegality of torture as an investigative tool and educate participants about the new 2010 laws, including the required elements of various crimes. The impact of these events is a greater understanding among the enforcers of the law, thus encouraging and enabling proper implementation of the law. The methodology is simple: by reducing the incorrect application of the law, unnecessary and illegal detention is also reduced. These training events are held in such high regard that in 2011 the Deputy Police Chief in Kampong Chhnang province specifically requested that additional trainings be conducted in his province to improve police practice. To date, IBJ has held 12 workshops and has trained 1,458 local justice stakeholders in eight separate provinces.

2. Also in partnership with the Ministry of Justice, IBJ Cambodia holds one-day Roundtable events. These events are

attended by judges, prosecutors, police, prison officials and members of civil society. The day is divided into two parts: dissemination and discussion of key provisions of the 2010 laws, followed by group discussions about problems facing Cambodia's justice system. At a recent event, the group was divided into two and each group was asked to come up with solutions to build better community trust in the justice system. This thought-provoking exercise resulted in candid discussions about corruption and trust of public officials. The overall objective of each Roundtable is to engage local justice stakeholders in creating changes in the justice system to enhance the delivery of legal services and strengthen justice stakeholder capacity. Since 2008, IBJ has held 17 such Roundtable events, training some 404 justice stakeholders in ten provinces.

The change in attitude is readily seen in the results of IBJ Cambodia's cases. The rate of torture that is documented in those cases is decreasing. In 2009, for example, IBJ Cambodia recorded a torture rate of 4.9 per cent of the number of cases handled. Today, this has been reduced to 1.3 per cent. This is significantly lower than the figures recorded by other local non-governmental organisations (NGOs), such as the Cambodian League for the Promotion and Defense of Human Rights (LICADHO) or the Cambodian Centre for Human Rights (CCHR). Through their prison and court monitoring programmes, both of these local NGOs record a current torture rate of about 7 per cent among those interviewees who were assessed (and who have not been represented by IBJ Cambodia (LICADHO, 2011: 12; CCHR, 2011: 35). This presents a striking measure of the impact of IBJ Cambodia's work: where the organisation is involved in a case, instances of torture have dropped markedly. However, due to the lack of privacy when interviewing clients in police stations and prisons, overall instances of torture are most likely under-reported. The prevalence of confessions in police custody presented at trial further supports the notion that torture is under-reported (CCHR, 2011: 35).

The significant increase in bail applications and proportionate sentencing practices that IBJ Cambodia lawyers are generating as programming expands throughout the country further reduces the risk of torture in police custody and prisons to a significant degree.

Comparative case study: Bourey and Phirun

In one of the most remote areas of Cambodia, 10 hours from Phnom Penh, Bourey is serving a 10-year prison sentence in Rattanakiri province. Six years ago, before the IBJ Cambodia office opened in Rattanakiri, 24 year old Bourey was convicted of murdering his violent and alcoholic uncle. When the government-appointed lawyer did not turn up to the trial, Bourey was tried and convicted without a lawyer. The circumstances surrounding the incident were not considered. There was no mention of the trauma to which the entire family had been subjected nor the precise life-threatening circumstances that led to the incident for which Bourey was convicted. He was sentenced to the maximum punishment available under Cambodian law. His wife and three children now struggle to survive.

This is in stark contrast to the case with similar facts in Prey Veng province. Phirun, 20, was also charged with murdering a violent alcoholic family member, his father. However, he was appointed an IBJ Cambodia lawyer, who made sure that during his trial the court took into account the circumstances of the crime. Phirun was able to describe the violent abuse he and his two younger siblings had repeatedly endured, and the trauma that this caused. He was also able to explain the conditions under which the crime actually took place. As a result of Phirun telling his story, he was sentenced to four years in prison: his lawyer had successfully argued for a reduced sentence.

The six-year difference in sentencing has a grave and dramatic impact not only for Bourey, but also for his wife and three children. These stories highlight the critical role that IBJ Cambodia lawyers play in the day-to-day administration of justice in Cambodia, and in the lives of real people. By providing early access to competent legal representation, IBJ Cambodia is ensuring that judges correctly implement the law by considering all the facts of a case. This also brings justice down to a very personal level.

In 2008, IBJ Cambodia was successful in 42 bail applications, compared with 141 in 2011. Similarly, in 2008 IBJ Cambodia received seven proportionate sentences, compared with 309 in 2011. The combination of a change in attitude, and IBJ Cambodia's growth to now cover 17 provinces, means that the organisation is directly impacting a larger portion of citizens who would otherwise be lost in the justice system and changing the behaviour of the justice system itself.

Early and competent legal counsel for the accused: training lawyers

'Having a defence lawyer present makes me work more carefully. I have to check my decisions to see if I have done something wrong. If there is no lawyer, then no one cares' (Meas Chanpyseth, Deputy Prosecutor, Phnom Penh, interview conducted 5 April 2012).

Following the complete destruction of the justice system, the first law school was re-established in 1994. With less than 20 years of established legal education and knowledge available in Cambodia, competent and skilled defence lawyers are in high demand. To meet this need, IBJ Cambodia and the Ministry of Justice collaborate to host skills and advocacy training sessions for all of IBJ Cambodia's defenders and investigators, as well as lawyers working for other legal NGOs. Topics include cross-examination, case theme and theory, evidence gathering and sentencing. To reinforce this skills training, IBJ Cambodia also disseminates the Criminal Procedure Code and Penal Code.

The impact that competent legal aid lawyers can have on a young life is quite often dramatic. One area where this is evident is in sentence mitigation, or proportionate sentencing. Sentence mitigation is the practice whereby a lawyer explains to the judge the circumstances surrounding the crime and other factors that should be taken into account to ensure that the punishment fits the totality of circumstances surrounding the crime. With access to competent legal representation, IBJ Cambodia lawyers ensure that the arbitrary sentencing practices of the past are abolished and that fair and just sentences are more regularly imposed. The stories of Bourey and Phirun in the accompanying box, regarding murder in self-defence, illustrate this point.

'The prisoners specifically request IBJ lawyers over other representation, based on recommendations from other prisoners' (Va Yorn, Chief of the Prey Veng Prison, interview conducted 25 May 2012).

Empowering individuals to assert their rights: street law

Greater citizen participation and empowerment in the justice sector also increases IBJ Cambodia's impact. Basic understanding of the law is severely lacking. It is not uncommon to find that ordinary Cambodians, especially from indigenous communities, do not understand what a lawyer does or how a lawyer may help them if they find themselves in trouble with the law.

To raise public awareness and educate the general population of its legal rights, IBJ Cambodia conducts street law campaigns throughout the provinces where it works. These half-day legal rights awareness events are critical to empowering ordinary citizens with the knowledge of their basic rights. Each event is coordinated through IBJ Cambodia's headquarters in Phnom Penh and includes the distribution of pamphlets, posters and other materials.

In organising these events, IBJ Cambodia's provincial lawyers work with local commune chiefs to identify key topics and invite participants from surrounding villages.

'The most important thing I learned today is to understand how a lawyer can help find justice for those who have been wrongly accused. I will share this information with the people of my village to make them aware of their rights' (Participant in Street Law campaign, Takeo Province, interview conducted 21 March 2012).

Materials distributed at these events address the following subject areas: 1) the right of the accused to counsel in all felony cases under the Criminal Procedure Code; 2) proper arrest and search procedures; 3) permissible time limits for pre-trial detention; and 4) the illegality of the use of torture against accused persons.

The street law campaigns not only enhance the legal rights awareness of Cambodia's largely illiterate population, particularly the indigenous groups in Rattanakiri and Mondulkiri provinces, but they also promote awareness of the availability of IBJ Cambodia's legal aid work. If citizens are not aware of this service, they easily may fall victim to corruption or abuse within the court system. To date, these legal rights awareness events have reached tens of thousands of ordinary Cambodians, many of whom have subsequently sought IBJ Cambodia's services.

Cost effectiveness

The Kingdom of Cambodia receives more than half its annual budget from foreign aid, making it one of the most foreign assistance dependent countries in the world (Fforde and Seidel, 2010: 4). In 2010, foreign aid totalled US$1.1 billion. The largest donors over the past two decades include the European Union (23.3 per cent), Japan (18.7 per cent), The Asian Development Bank (10 per cent), and international NGOs (8.8 per cent), with government and administration (including the legal and judicial sectors), health, transport, and education sectors receiving the majority of the funds (Royal Government of Cambodia, 2010: 9).

Despite or perhaps due to the overwhelming amount of aid money pouring into the country, development efforts in Cambodia are highly fragmented (Chanboreth and Hach, 2008: 20), with recipients having a low degree of input or ownership of programmes and projects (van de Sande, 2010: 49; Hubbard, 2002: 17). Top level political will also remains a key obstacle to meaningful reform in many sectors. The results are wasted efforts, project duplication, lack of development coordination, low degree of local community involvement and, ultimately, reduced and unsustainable impact.

IBJ Cambodia understands the complexity of this situation, and has designed its approach precisely to navigate these hurdles, working where both the need for reform and political will are greatest. It engages directly at the local level, training and employing Cambodian lawyers to provide defence to indigent clients, and training and empowering those local justice officials who are most interested in achieving tangible reform. All programming and strategic decisions about where and how to engage are directed by the local team in response to well understood conditions on the ground. This leads to an implementation style that provides enhanced local relevance and much greater credibility in the eyes of local stakeholders.

IBJ Cambodia's programmes, beginning at the local level, are designed to then trickle up over time, simultaneously creating a sustainable and replicable model while generating grassroots demand to which policy makers respond. This is much more than a simple preference about how to work: compared with larger-funded externally driven top-down interventions, this bottom-up, locally oriented approach delivers much more locally relevant and sustainable results in the current political environment.

Year	Annual operating cost for Cambodia US$	Total number of clients	Number of bail applications approved	Number of reduced sentences	Number of acquittals and dismissals
2008	52,805	60	42	7	10
2009	119,267	517	185	37	86
2010	184,584	1044	215	343	181
2011	244,541	963	141	309	71
Total	**601,197**	**3,001**	**617**	**735**	**354**

Table 1

Financial comparisons among assistance programmes are difficult, as IBJ Cambodia is the only NGO in the country that provides legal aid to Cambodian defendants on a broad scale. However, a hallmark of IBJ Cambodia's efforts has always been a low cost, locally driven and owned programme orientation. For the years 2010 and 2011, IBJ Cambodia's entire budget was US$184,584 and US$244,541, respectively. This contrasts sharply with typically much larger donor interventions in the justice sector.

Presented another way, IBJ Cambodia's cost of delivering justice on a case-by-case, person-by-person basis, is remarkably low. The organisation has represented over 3,000 clients since 2008 (see Table 1), or around 20 per cent of the number of currently incarcerated individuals in the Cambodian prison system.[7] Since 2009, the average cost of providing legal aid to each client has ranged from US$177-254 (see Graph 1.5). Similarly, the total cost of operating each DRC is around US$17,000 annually, or US$2,317 per month – figures that include salaries, as well as lawyer and police trainings, roundtables, and street law costs.

---

7 LICADHO, 'Cambodian Prison Overcrowding Crisis Only Gets Worse', 4 July 2011. For the full report, see: http://www.licadho-cambodia.org/reports/files/154LICADHORep ortPrisonStillBeyondCapacityEng.pdf.

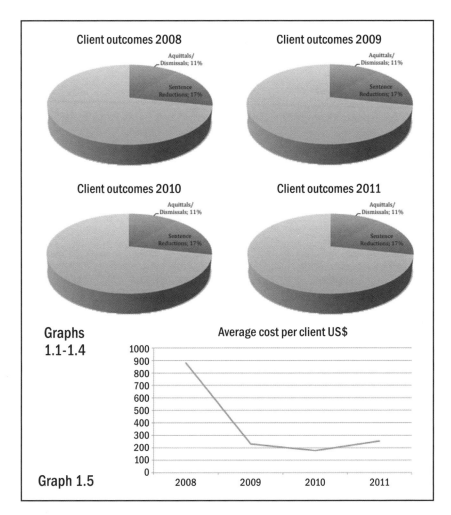

Graphs 1.1-1.4

Graph 1.5

IBJ's cost-effective methodology directly stems from its grass-roots approach. This includes local management and control of all programming, employing local staff, establishing a permanent presence in the provinces to increase local impact and reduce travel costs, and utilising international expertise on a volunteer basis as needed. This combines to keep administrative costs as low as possible while maintaining competitive salaries for the local team. IBJ Cambodia's holistic approach to improving access to justice – direct representation complemented by lawyer and police trainings, roundtables, and street law campaigns – builds local ownership and commitment towards a national legal aid system, thus ensuring long-term impact on a national scale. As a result, this approach is not only cost-effective in terms of representing individual clients, but also achieves important, sustainable results for the future of the Cambodian justice system.

Expanding the IBJ Cambodia model: a 12-year plan

The past ten years have seen positive changes in the Cambodian criminal justice system. Justice stakeholders from both civil society and the justice sector now speak about a greater awareness among police, local justice officials, and even the general population on issues related to legal rights and the proper role of the criminal justice system. Most importantly, IBJ Cambodia lawyers working throughout the county have been accepted by the broader justice system and are able to effectively protect the rights of the accused.

IBJ Cambodia has put the pieces in place to make Cambodia a global model for universal access to legal aid and the protection of due process rights. However, much remains to be done. In collaboration with the Ministry of Justice, IBJ Cambodia recently has identified the key elements for a sustainable and state-sponsored legal aid system to be put into place over the next 12 years, including:

- A need to develop nationwide legal aid services to all courts.
- Continue capacity building and training of criminal defence lawyers and justice sector officials.
- Further increase early access to counsel through collaboration with local and national justice stakeholders.
- Expand rights awareness campaigns to reach out to all individuals in Cambodia.

The growth over the past 20 years from six to over 600 lawyers has had a substantial impact on the functioning of the justice system. A recently trained legal aid defender put it like this:

'The main purpose for a lawyer is to help the people to become aware of the law and to provide legal assistance. The lawyers allow for a right to a fair trial and not to be tortured. In the future, I hope that I can contribute to the legal justice system by providing access to a lawyer. I especially want to help the accused get out of pre-trial detention and to reduce torture' (Interview conducted 7 April 2012).

However there is still a dire shortage of properly trained and supported legal aid lawyers in the country, particularly in remote locations. Increasing the number of lawyers available to provide legal aid services remains IBJ Cambodia's first priority towards increasing access to justice throughout Cambodia.

In addition to increasing the number of legal aid lawyers, it is necessary to continue to disseminate the law to justice stakeholders in order to improve their understanding and interpretation of the law. As the capacity of these justice stakeholders increases, so does their appreciation of their own role in the country's transition to a rule of law system. Thus, by ensuring local ownership of changes to the functioning of the justice system, IBJ Cambodia is fostering genuinely sustainable reform.

Efforts to educate and empower local citizens about their legal rights must also be accelerated, slowly but continually building a sense of trust among citizens in the impartial operation of the justice system. And, of course, all of these efforts will be underscored by an expanded legal aid presence throughout the country, ensuring that every citizen who is accused has early access to counsel, whenever or wherever they may need it.

All of these actions, scaled up to the point of country-wide presence, will allow IBJ Cambodia to move towards its ultimate goal: transferring a fully functioning, nationwide legal aid system to government ownership and operation. Achieving this will undoubtedly remain challenging for years to come. Like many NGOs, IBJ Cambodia constantly struggles to find sufficient resources. The work IBJ Cambodia does is considered by some to be mundane and there are many critics who dismiss the possibility that there will be any significant improvement to the justice sector in Cambodia. But IBJ Cambodia sees otherwise, and is continually moving towards its goal by opening offices in new provinces, obtaining the MoU with the Ministry of Justice, representing more and more citizens, and improving access to justice for the most vulnerable Cambodians.

Conclusions

There is clear evidence that IBJ's grassroots approach in Cambodia, especially its local orientation to reforming the justice system, has produced tangible results over the past four years. The link between improved access to justice and improved protection of human rights on a systematic basis is also clear. Most importantly, the IBJ Cambodia model demonstrates how a holistic, grassroots approach to change – by simultaneously engaging citizens and justice stakeholders, combining case-by-case legal aid representation with education and policy level discussions – can produce results that are both cost-effective and sustainable.

The United Nations recently recognised the fact that providing citizens access to defence lawyers and legal aid directly correlates with improved protection of human rights.[8] IBJ Cambodia has understood this all along. Cambodia now is at a tipping point. Achieving universal access to a defence lawyer and government ownership of legal aid in Cambodia will offer a clear example of how countries can take practical steps to transition from non-functioning legal systems to protecting human rights. More than this, they will see that what might formerly have seemed impossible is now happening, providing strength and courage to all those in other countries facing similar struggles today.

References

Cambodian Centre for Human Rights (CCHR). 'Third Bi-Annual Report Fair Trial Rights: One Year Progress'. Phnom Penh: Cambodian Centre for Human Rights, 2011 (released January 2012).

Cambodian League for the Promotion and Defense of Human Rights (LICADHO). 'Protecting and Defending Human Rights in Cambodia', Activity Report January. Phnom Penh: LICADHO, June 2011.

Cambodian League for the Promotion and Defense of Human Rights (LICADHO). 'Beyond Capacity: Cambodia's Exploding Prison Population and Correction Center 4'. Phnom Penh: LICADHO, 2010.

Cambodian League for the Promotion and Defense of Human Rights (LICADHO). 'Prison Conditions in Cambodia 2005 and 2006: One Day in the Life'. Phnom Penh: LICADHO, 2007.

Cambodian League for the Promotion and Defense of Human Rights

---

8 *See: United Nations Economic and Social Council, 'Commission on Crime Prevention and Criminal Justice, Twenty-first Session: Use and application of United Nations standards and norms in crime prevention and criminal justice', 25 April 2012.*

(LICADHO). 'Human Rights and Cambodia's Prisons: Health in Prisons 2002 and 2003'. Phnom Penh: LICADHO, 2004.

Chanboreth, Ek and Sok Hach. 'Aid Effectiveness in Cambodia'. Washington, DC: Wolfensohn Center for Development, Brookings Institution, 2008.

Fforde, Adam and Katrin Seidel. 'Donor Playground Cambodia?: What a Look at Aid and Development in Cambodia Confirms and What It May Imply'. Berlin: Heinrich Boll Stiftung, 2010.

Government of Australia, Scoping Mission. 'Australia's Assistance to Criminal Justice Reform in Cambodia: Strategic Framework Document'. Canberra: Australian Agency for International Development, May 2007.

Hammarberg, Thomas (Special Representative of the Secretary-General for Human Rights in Cambodia). 'Situation of Human Rights in Cambodia', Report to the 53rd Session of the Commission on Human Rights, Geneva, 2 April 1997.

Hubbard, Michael. 'Cambodia: A Country Case Study'. OECD (DAC Task Force on Donor Practices), November 2002.

Hor, Peng, Kong, Phallack and Jorg, Menzel (Eds). Introduction to Cambodian Law. Phnom Penh: Konrad Adenauer Stiftung, 2012.

Royal Government of Cambodia and the Cambodian Rehabilitation and Development Board of the Council for the Development for Cambodia. 'The Cambodia Aid Effectiveness Report'. Phnom Penh: Cambodian Rehabilitation and Development Board, 2010.

Un, Kheang. 'The Judicial System and Democratization in Post-Conflict Cambodia' in Beyond Democracy in Cambodia: Political Reconstruction in a Post-Conflict Society. Joakim Ojendal and Mona Lilja (Eds), Copenhagen: NIAS Press, Series: Democracy in Asia, Volume 12, 2009.

van de Sande, Ann. 'Challenges to the Effective Operation of Local NGOs in Cambodia: Ownership, NGO-isation, Strategy and Knowledge of Local NGOs in Cambodia'. Netherlands: Radboud University Nijmegen, June 2010.

Creating grassroots accountability in Timor Leste: Luta Hamutuk

by Victoria Fanggidae [1]

Staying with the theme of good governance, the fifth case study on Luta Hamutuk in Timor Leste addresses government accountability and transparency. This case study shows that efforts to strengthen formal state anti-corruption institutions can benefit from grassroots participation in local-level monitoring of government infrastructure projects, by playing a complementary role in reducing corruption and improving service delivery. Citizens are also empowered to exercise their rights, and space is thus created for citizen-state engagement in dealing with development challenges. Not only does this approach reflect the value that Local First accords to more responsive civil society-government relations, but the nationwide network of volunteer local monitors that is crucial to the success of Luta Hamutuk likewise exemplifies a Local First principle. With high levels of corruption throughout Timor Leste, Luta Hamutuk's locally led approach to accountability and transparency in this oil-rich country can offer an effective model for adaptation in other oil- and mineral-rich countries around the world – assuming its relevance is first tested.

Accountability in post-conflict Timor Leste

After a long history of violent conflict, Timor Leste embraces its first decade of independence in 2012. Reconstructing the country's physical and social infrastructures is a priority because of the staggering social and economic challenges it encounters. Building a large number of infrastructures that either were destroyed or did not exist in the pre-independence era comes with risks. Whether they are managed by government agencies or private contractors, these various infrastructure projects are prone to corruption and

1 The author gratefully acknowledges Luta Hamutuk staff members, especially Mericio Akara (director), and Siobhan O'Shea and Claire Schouten from Integrity Action for their support and cooperation in providing information for and feedback on the text. This text is also based on a range of internal Luta Hamutuk documents and reports; ie, activity and progress reports, as well as annual reports and other relevant information.

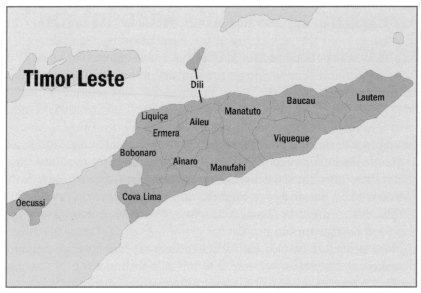

Map showing impact of project

misappropriation of resources. Therefore, improving transparency and accountability is critical to curb corruption in such projects.

About half of the nation's 1.1 million people live in poverty, are unemployed and illiterate. Almost 70 per cent of the youth population is jobless, which may pose a serious latent security risk. Food insecurity is prevalent, which contributes to the large number of malnourished children and high levels of child and maternal mortality. Economic growth and access to public services are hindered by poor infrastructures and public facilities that are a result of past conflict and colonial legacies.[2]

Economically, the country sources almost 90 per cent of its income from petroleum revenues, making it one of the world's most oil-dependent economies. In 2012, the Timor Leste Petroleum Fund is set to grow to almost US$10 billion. Combined with significant levels of international aid (slightly over US$260 million of foreign aid was disbursed in 2011),[3] the country's economic growth has reached an average of 7 to 8 per cent since 2009, matching the

2 *When the Portuguese left in 1974, about 90 per cent of the population were illiterate, and there was only one high school in Timor Leste. When Timor Leste gained independence from Indonesia in 1999, 80 per cent of the infrastructure was destroyed, 50 per cent of population remained illiterate and public administration was in collapse (Bria and Jorgesen, 2011).*

3 *See: http://www.aidtransparency.gov.tl/.*

GDP growth of its Asian neighbours. However, the impact of this growth rate on the well-being of the population is minimal.

Although its dependency on oil revenues increases the risks of corruption and rent seeking,[4] the Government of Timor Leste has complied with the Extractive Industries Transparency Initiative (EITI) by promulgating the Petroleum Fund Law in 2005.[5] Under this law, the government established the Petroleum Fund, where oil revenue is deposited in order to secure the national budget for development. To ensure accountability, withdrawals from the fund must be approved by three agencies: the Investment Advisory Board, the Ministry of Planning and Finance and the Central Bank of Timor Leste. A threshold of 3 per cent was set on how much money can be used for the annual budget.[6]

The government also publishes its annual budget and expenditures for public scrutiny, as well as has established a set of transparency portals[7] in order to be accountable to its citizens and donors.

For a newly established state, Timor Leste has relatively advanced institutional arrangements on anti-corruption. For example, the penal code regulates economic crime, the Civil Service Statute of 2004 sets a framework and code of ethics for public servants, and Law No. 7/2004, promulgated by the national parliament, established an Ombudsman for Human Rights and Justice (Provedoria dos Direitos Humanos e Justiça) that included an anti-corruption division. In 2009, this division was replaced with the Anti-Corruption Commission (Comissão Anti-Corrupção; CAC). Timor Leste has also signed the United Nations Convention Against Corruption. These laws and obligations, combined with a free press and strong political opposition parties, indicate that this young nation

---

4 *Rent seeking is usually defined as an attempt by individuals or groups to create income opportunities or to gain economic privileges from government projects through political activity.*

5 *The law was amended in August 2011 primarily to allow more flexibility and diversification of asset allocation in order to gain a greater return on investments, but this also exposed the fund to more risks and volatility.*

6 *However, in 2008, the government withdrew more than 3 per cent, with parliamentary approval, claiming this was necessary for the increasing government spending, in particular for public works projects. Nearly US$294 million was to be withdrawn from the Petroleum Fund. See: http://www.laohamutuk.org/econ/MYBU08/RDTLMYBU08.htm.*

7 *In 2011 and 2012, the Ministry of Finance launched four transparency portals. These are public websites where people can access information on: 1) the state budget; 2) aid in Timor Leste; 3) e-procurement; and 4) government progress on priority projects and programmes. For additional information, see: http://www.transparency.gov.tl/english.html.*

has the three main ingredients necessary to take an anti-corruption agenda onboard (Management Systems International, 2009: 3).

Despite this, the people of Timor Leste want tougher enforcement on corruption cases. In practice, these state institutions appear to be less effective.[8] In particular, they lack the necessary institutional capacities and human resources to perform at the level expected by the citizens of Timor Leste and relevant external actors (ie, the donor community).[9] Nepotism, graft and a rent-seeking culture are prevalent among bureaucrats and top officials and such practices are commonly reported in the media.[10] The use of different languages for official documents poses difficulties in terms of access to information and disclosure. In addition, weak oversight roles in parliament and the Ministry of Finance, among others, hamper anti-corruption efforts (*ibid*, 15). As a result, the Corruption Perception Index in Timor Leste is high: 2.4 on a 10-point scale, and ranked 143 out of 183 countries.[11]

Whilst efforts to establish and strengthen formal state institutions responsible for anti-corruption are in progress, a promising approach to increase the accountability and transparency of government policies and programmes is through grassroots participation in local-level monitoring. A community-driven accountability mechanism that monitors government projects, such as schools, hospitals, roads and veterans' housing construction projects and their management can provide an alternative avenue for reducing corruption, as well as improving public service delivery in general. Through participation in monitoring government policies and programmes, local people exercise their rights as citizens in holding the government accountable.

Civil society organisations in Timor Leste, such as Luta Hamutuk, play a pivotal role in building this capacity and creating space for citizen-state engagement in post-conflict Timor Leste as the nation works to address its daunting human development challenges.

---

8 *GlobalPost, 12 April 2010. 'Analysis: Tough Task to Tackle Corruption in East Timor'. See: http://www.globalpost.com/dispatch/asia/100330/east-timor-leste-corruption.*
9 *This lack of capacity is due to the low levels of literacy and numeracy skills, which severely affect many public sectors.*
10 *For instance, in 2010, the deputy prime minister resigned over corruption after he alleged that there was rampant graft, corruption, collusion and nepotism at the Ministry of Finance and in the context of government purchases.*
11 *See Transparency International website: http://www.transparency.org/country#TLS.*

Empowering communities and providing an interface for citizen-state engagement

Established in 2005 by a group of activists passionate about ensuring an accountable and participatory development process in Timor Leste, Luta Hamutuk is a national civil society organisation committed to economic justice and public participation with regard to the values of democracy, equality and transparency. This is achieved through empowering citizens, influencing government policies, sharing lessons with other civil society groups and improving state services to the people of Timor Leste by building institutional capacities.

Luta Hamutuk believes that local people best understand the specific needs and circumstances of their communities because they live in or near these project sites. Thus their voices must be counted. However, before an infrastructure development project is undertaken, communities often have no way to channel their concerns and observations about the quality and quantity of projects that are being built in their areas. Luta Hamutuk aims to address this problem by providing a variety of ways for communities to convey their concerns to those who are responsible for infrastructure projects, enabling them to engage with key stakeholders in order to foster greater accountability at local, district and national levels.

The majority of the people in Timor Leste live in rural poverty, remote from the centres of power in urban Dili, the capital. In addition to a combination of poverty and a dominant culture defined in terms of feudal relations and kinship ties, many people in Timor Leste lack access to both knowledge and those who hold power. For Luta Hamutuk, then, empowering local people is the most important aspect of their work.

At the practical level, citizens are entitled to monitor whether or not the government demonstrates the principles of good governance (ie, transparency, accountability, and rule of law) in implementing its policies and programmes. These values are manifest in the three primary areas of work on which Luta Hamutuk focuses:[12]
- **Budget transparency programme:** Luta Hamutuk examines the state budget and shares its findings with affected communities.
- **Oil transparency programme:** Luta Hamutuk monitors govern-

12 *For more information, see: http://www.lutahamutukinstitute.org/about/program/.*

ment implementation of EITI and shares its findings with both local communities and relevant national stakeholders.

- **Community networking initiative:** Luta Hamutuk coordinates and trains focal points, including community monitoring of infrastructure projects.

The first two programmes have been active since the organisation was first established, whilst the latter commenced in 2009.

Luta Hamutuk has worked in partnership with Integrity Action (formerly Tiri) through their Network for Integrity in Reconstruction since 2008. Both organisations have a similar approach to community-driven accountability and integrity building. Integrity Action partnered with Cafod and the Revenue Watch Institute to support Luta Hamutuk's strategic plans. All three organisations work closely with Luta Hamutuk to develop relevant tools and approaches, as well as support the organisation in reporting and strategic planning. Through this partnership, Luta Hamutuk has further developed community-driven accountability work in Timor Leste, bridging the gap between the state and its citizens.

The aim of promoting and strengthening community monitoring capacities is to empower local people to demand government accountability. The theory of change that informs Luta Hamutuk's work is straightforward: providing information and knowledge to local people will increase their awareness of their rights and responsibilities in the state-citizen relationship, which will encourage them to take action and become involved in monitoring and interacting with government and private contractors. Consequently, government will be more accountable and responsive to the needs and demands of its citizens (see Figure 1).

Luta Hamutuk plays the role of catalyst and facilitator in these three stages of the change process. In stage 1, its role is to provide information and knowledge that otherwise would not be available to local people. This ranges from information about the state budget and oil revenues to local infrastructure projects. In stage 2, to enable local people to take action, Luta Hamutuk provides them with necessary capacities and resources, such as training on data collection, report writing and advocacy. In stage 3, Luta Hamutuk engages with and pressurises the government to perform its duties, as well as be more responsive and accountable to the citizens of Timor Leste (see Figure 2).

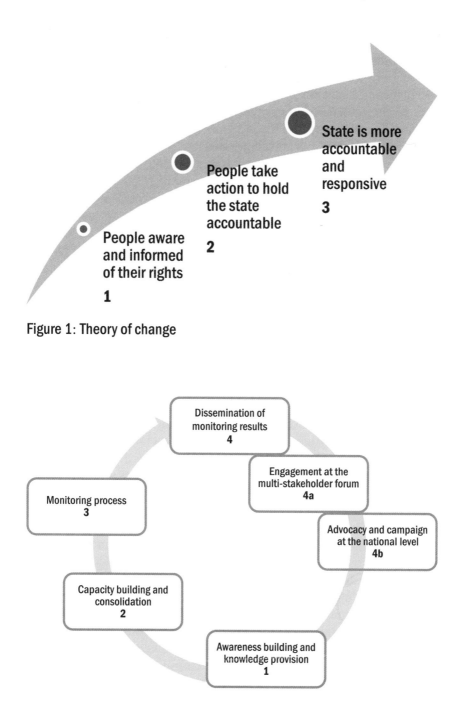

Figure 1: Theory of change

Figure 2: Luta Hamutuk community-driven monitoring process

The Luta Hamutuk approach

Awareness building and knowledge provision

Building awareness and providing knowledge are essential to the work of Luta Hamutuk. This is primarily done through community briefings, with staff initially identifying suitable villages to approach. These include, for example, villages that do not have or have limited access to information or remote villages lacking access to transportation. Such villages are more vulnerable to exploitation and corruption precisely because of their remoteness.

An initial approach is made to local leaders and other existing civil society organisations, such as youth and women's groups. Once Luta Hamutuk has built trust and good relationships with these groups, the most suitable villages are chosen in which to hold community briefings.

The main purpose of a community briefing is to share information and facilitate discussion on issues like the national budget, the petroleum fund, as well as government infrastructure projects and public services in their area. In addition to becoming aware of recent developments and debates in the country, local residents acquire a basis of knowledge for their subsequent monitoring activities of projects in their communities. Community briefings also serve as a forum for local residents to give feedback on and participate in the reconstruction process underway in Timor Leste.

A typical community briefing agenda includes the presentation of *faktus informasaun* (fact sheets) about national and local issues relevant to the community, which are prepared by Luta Hamutuk staff. Fact sheets focus on budget allocations for infrastructure projects in their area, the national budget, and oil and gas issues. This is followed by a discussion session to address questions from local residents. Often, this part of the meeting triggers critical thinking about government plans and policies, especially as this relates to local developments and projects.

This is reflected in comments from two participants at a community briefing, held in April 2008 in the village of Maumeta Vila (Atauro Island) in the district of Dili. For example, as Patricio de Jesus, a villager, says, 'It is clear that Timor Leste is a state said to be rich with natural resource but we, the people, don't feel it since the government do not realise its programs just like what they had said during campaign' (Luta Hamutuk activity report, 2008). Joanina, a midwife from the same village, explains:

> *'We had known nothing about the state budget and its function, therefore Luta Hamutuk's presence today is very important. Many problems had happened here, so we wonder if the government have any regulation regarding contract employees. Power abuse has been happening since many of health equipments within Atauro Hospital have been used as if they are private things by certain people' (ibid).*

Focal points

Community briefings are also an opportunity for Luta Hamutuk staff to identify and recruit potential focal points from among the meeting participants. Focal points are local residents who make a voluntary commitment to serve as community organisers. Some of the focal points have full-time jobs. They may come from youth and student groups, and women's organisations. They are teachers, village leaders, farmers – anyone interested in volunteering their time, playing a role as an active citizen and willing to learn for that end.

Prior to commencing their work as focal points, Luta Hamutuk (with support from Integrity Action) conducts capacity building workshops so that these volunteers are adequately equipped to collect evidence that is credible and verifiable, conduct proper monitoring exercises, write reports and engage with local leaders and national policymakers. Coordination and building good relationships with local authorities, such as village chiefs, is important for focal points in order to get their support on monitoring activities and avoid resistance. To date, Luta Hamutuk has trained 146 voluntary focal points who live in all of the 13 districts of the country.

In the pipeline of Luta Hamutuk's community-based work, the focal points serve as the link between the organisation (including the Dili-based policy community) and the local community.[13] Focal points are responsible for facilitating ongoing community briefings, which includes preparing briefing materials in cooperation with Luta Hamutuk staff and mobilising participants to attend the meetings. Community briefings are generally held once a month (12 times a year), in various districts of Timor Leste, with approximately 25-30 participants at each session.

---

13 For a full description on the role of focal points, see Bria and Jorgensen (2011).

Opportunities from becoming a Community Focal Point (Julio Gomez, 22 years old)

Julio is in his last semester as a university student at the National University of Timor Leste, majoring in Community Development. He first learned about Luta Hamutuk during a community briefing in his village, Suco Fatumasi. He was selected to become the village focal point and attended the first focal point training in 2010. Now he actively engages in monitoring projects in his village and other villages in the sub-district of Bazartete through the Infrastructure Monitoring Committee there. As a student, he has to divide his time between studying and undertaking monitoring work in his capacity as a focal point.

When asked why he wanted to become a focal point, Julio said, 'Here I can have much information on the state budget, development projects in my area and other info that I can share with people in my village. Working as a focal point also supports my studies at the university because I can gain some groundwork experiences apart from studying.'

In response to a question about the most significant change in his life as a focal point during the past year, Julio replied, 'As a student from a humble family in the village, I have never gotten the chance to meet high ranking government officers and interview them about the projects in my village. But after I became a focal point and with facilitation from Luta Hamutuk staff, I can meet and talk to them about problems in my village.'

Source: Luta Hamutuk, 2011: 20.

Monitoring committees

When local circumstances allow, a monitoring committee is established. To do so requires good relationships and trust between community members and the local authorities, as well as focal points with sufficient capacity in the area (at the sub-district or district level) to monitor and engage with key stakeholders. A monitoring committee is a multi-stakeholder forum comprised of community members (such as village chiefs, focal points, youth and women's representatives), representatives from local government, chiefs of sectoral offices (health, education or public works), the chief of police at sub-district or district level, and one or two Luta Hamutuk staff. Selection criteria for membership in a monitoring committee are based on willingness to carry out tasks on a voluntary basis, the capacity to undertake the necessary duties and the specific sector that a monitoring committee member represents. A committee usually has an average of ten members.

Luta Hamutuk established its first monitoring committee, the Monitoring and Supervision Committee for Infrastructure Development Project (Komite de Monitorizasaun e Supervisaun Projectu Desenvolvimentu Infrastruktura District Lautem, or KMSPDI), in Lautem district. Establishing KMSPDI was part of a pilot programme initiated by Luta Hamutuk in 2007 and to date there are now a total of three monitoring committees, which are in the districts of Aileu (Remeixa), Liquica (Bazartete) and Lautem (Los Palos). These committees focus on local projects ranging from road rehabilitation to developing schools and improving healthcare facilities.

Monitoring committees normally meet once a month. Focal points share their monitoring findings and the status of the projects that they are monitoring. Committee members discuss how to follow up on findings, including whether any problems or challenges that have been encountered can be solved at the local level (eg, dealing with the private contractors or service providers themselves), or whether it is necessary to engage in advocacy activities at the national level. In the absence of any official complaint mechanisms at the local level, the monitoring committees also serve as a channel for complaints.

For instance, problems are often raised during formal development meetings, such as a Local Development Programme Meeting in a village. The focal points or village chief identify a priority problem and then monitoring, data collection and verification is undertaken. The problem that is raised is also substantiated by consulting local people, especially those who are the intended beneficiaries of the infrastructure project (eg, parents, farmers, patients, students, veterans, and so on). Once data has been gathered, the monitoring committee follows up with appropriate action. A good example of this process is the case of inadequate school facilities for students in Maumeta village, Bazartete sub-district, Liquica district.

Resuming effective class activities in Maumeta village, Bazartete Sub-District, Liquica district

This project began after the community focal points attended a meeting about the local development programme. At this meeting, the chief of Maumeta village pointed out that the primary school there had no basic facilities, such as chairs, tables and blackboards. Having discussed the problem with him, the focal points and the village chief went to see the condition of the school building and verify relevant information.The school consisted of three rooms: one for teachers, of which there were two, and two classrooms. The students had to sit on the floor during their classes because there were no chairs or tables. Teachers also had difficulties explaining their lesson plans because there were no blackboards.

These findings were explained and discussed during a monthly monitoring committee meeting in Bazartete. The committee later decided to send a letter to the Ministry of Education to address the problem. The letter was drafted in consultation with the teachers, the village chief, the youth chief and the parents of the students. Luta Hamutuk then facilitated the submission of the letter to the Ministry of Education. One and a half months later, officers from the Department of Education visited the school to verify the information in the letter and agreed to fulfil the request for basic equipment. Chairs, tables and blackboards are now provided to the school and have directly benefited 152 primary students in Maumeta Village.

Source: Luta Hamutuk, 2011: 18.

Disseminating evidence: advocacy and media campaigns

Depending on the circumstances related to a problem, facts collected by Luta Hamutuk are used for advocacy purposes through press conferences, which are then publicised in national TV, radio and newspapers. Luta Hamutuk chose press releases and press conferences as a key advocacy method for bringing local issues to the national level because they have found media to be an effective method to get publicity for local issues, which are often marginalised. Press releases and press conferences are based on issues that are monitored by Luta Hamutuk, and which are considered important for getting attention from both communities and government. Luta Hamutuk has developed good relationships with the national media in Timor Leste. In particular, the organisation maintains frequent contact with Radio Nacional Timor Leste and Diario Nacional, a widely read national newspaper, with distribution to district areas.

For example, take the case of a veterans' housing project and a Luta Hamutuk advocacy and media campaign. During its monitoring and investigation phase of the project, Luta Hamutuk conducted three press conferences in the districts of Manatuto, Lautem and Dili between August and September 2008. They also arranged for community radio stations to conduct two interviews on the same topic. The press release was also issued to the president, the prime minister, the national parliament, the State Secretary of State of Veterans and Combatants Affairs (SEAVAC), the media and relevant non-governmental organisations (NGOs) in Timor Leste. Based on its findings, which were published in the press release, Luta Hamutuk then held formal and informal meetings with SEAVAC, as well as hearings with the procurement companies and members of parliament. After press conferences and special interviews with national television and community radio stations on the topic of veterans' housing, both the media and the public started to pay more attention to what had happened during the construction phase and how the government would respond to such problems.

These problems included, for instance, a lack of coordination between national and local government about the construction planning. The number of houses that were built did not match with number of veterans in the area; eg, in Lautem district, only 19 houses were built, whereas there were 75 veterans in the district. The houses were also too small (just six square metres) to accommodate veterans' families. In Liquica district, some of the houses were not newly built, but rather were old buildings from the Indonesian era that were renovated. Finally, some houses in Lautem district and Iliomar sub-district were built in unsafe locations prone to flooding and landslides. Following the various meetings and hearings about these problems, Luta Hamutuk produced a *faktus informasaun*, which was published on a daily basis for one week in Diario Nacional.

Luta Hamutuk often succeeds in its role in the community because of its reputation as a prominent watchdog organisation in Timor Leste. During community briefings, community members and local authorities frequently reveal their dissatisfaction with and

---

Road rehabilitation links Cowa village and Balibo sub-district

When Luta Hamutuk had a community briefing in Cowa Village in March 2009, local authorities and community residents reported that a road rehabilitation project in their village had serious problems related to the quality of the work. Luta Hamutuk studied the project documents and found that a report from the Secretary of State for Public Works claimed that the project had been 100 per cent implemented and completed in December 2008.

However, the facts that were gathered indicated that the project was far from complete, indicating that there were discrepancies between government reports and the facts on the ground. Based on this finding, Luta Hamutuk sent letters to the Minister of Infrastructure, relevant ombudsmen, the national parliament and the prime minister. The letter and corresponding press release provoked an official investigation into the Cowa road project by the ombudsmen and police. As a result, the Ministry of Infrastructure instructed the Secretary of State for Public Works to continue the Cowa road rehabilitation project, which is now ongoing at the time of publication.

Source: Luta Hamutuk, 2010b.

---

suspicions about local infrastructure projects that might indicate problems with corruption. This preliminary information is then followed up by Luta Hamutuk and the focal points through investigation and document reviews. The results are then brought to the national government and disseminated through media, as illustrated in the above example.

The effectiveness of a community-driven monitoring approach

The community-driven monitoring approach is proven to be an effective and highly relevant way for Luta Hamutuk to facilitate and enable local communities to solve the problems they encounter in the post-conflict reconstruction setting of Timor Leste. Supporting factors to the effectiveness of this approach are the methods Luta Hamutuk uses to build community awareness, the active involvement and tireless effort of the focal points as representatives of their local communities, the quality of the organisation's advocacy materials and fact sheets, the presence of multi-stakeholder forums and the good public profile that Luta Hamutuk has developed as a facilitator of this approach.

In particular, the community briefings that Luta Hamutuk holds to build awareness of citizen rights, entitlements and responsibilities has proven to be very cost effective. For example, such meetings mostly rely on voluntary contributions from the community, who work to prepare the meetings. Luta Hamutuk only provides a small amount of money for snacks and/or meals, staff transport and telephone, amounting to an average cost of US$200 per briefing. Although increased levels of knowledge, which are measured in post-test evaluations of the materials that Luta Hamutuk presents, average around 50 per cent, this rate of success is understandable because the information shared with the communities is generally entirely new to them. Nonetheless, sharing knowledge is an important beginning, especially for those who live far away from the centre of information in Dili. As the village chief from Leorema, Mr Leandro, explains, this knowledge is 'a candle that lights the whole village' (Luta Hamutuk, 2010a: 16).

Focal points are the backbone of Luta Hamutuk's approach to community-based monitoring because they serve as the main contact between Luta Hamutuk and local communities, local authorities, civil society organisations and other key stakeholders, such as the private contractors who implement infrastructure development projects. Focal points do not receive a salary, but are provided with transportation costs and per diems, in case they need to travel away from their village (eg, for training or other advocacy activities). Their tireless efforts and dedication exceed what they receive in terms of material benefit. A training session, such as an advocacy workshop for one group of 30 to 40 focal points, costs approximately US$4,000 per training. After their training, focal points undertake most of the monitoring and advocacy work in their communities, which improves the effectiveness of this work because they are local people who know and better understand their local situations.

With the presence of active and well-trained focal points, along with the willing cooperation of local authorities, establishing and running a monitoring committee is much smoother. Participants in

Table 1: Reconstruction projects monitored by Luta Hamutuk and focal points 2011

	Project name	Project value US$	Implementer
1	Construction of clean water, Ulmera village	70,000	Nalos Unipessoal
2	Construction of water supply, Metagou village	120,000	Milcha Unipessoal Lda
3	Construction of health service post (Sisca) Maumeta Lau, Maumeta village	33,000	Xefe Aldeia
4	Construction of primary school, Hunbuti, Tibar village	35,000	Espada Unipessoal Lda
5	Construction of water supply solar panel system, Leorema village	180,000	Not available
6	Construction of irrigation, Aileu village	94,000	TAOID Unipessoal Lda
7	Construction of irrigation, Seloi Malere village	247,000	Valmar Unipessoal Lda
8	Rural road rehabilitation between Lokmau-village and Ulu-Acumau	15,000	Remexio Construction Unipessoal Lda
9	Construction of clean water pump solar panel system, Maneluma sub-village, Madabeno village, Laulara	100,000	Bilum-Hatu Unipessoal Lda
10	Construction of primary school branch (EPF), Lismori	29,000	Barudu Matak Construction Unipessoal Lda
11	Construction of irrigation, Manutasi village	40,000	Soka-Mau'ulu Unipessoal Lda
12	Canalization of water supply, Raebuti Udo sub-village, Manutasi village	23,000	Sera–Tai Unipessoal Lda
13	Construction of the pre-secondary school (EB EPS), Ladi	199,892	Unidade Unipessoal Lda
14	Construction of health services post (Sisca), Tutuala village	12,573	Pitileti Unipessoal Lda
15	Clean water canalization, Tutuala village	51,034	Jaco Unipessoal

Source: Luta Hamutuk.

these multi-stakeholder committees are generally positive in their feedback about Luta Hamutuk, especially because this approach allows them to effectively express their concerns about improving the infrastructure projects in their areas. Overall, monitoring committees have served to improve the quality of infrastructure projects in their areas.

The typical cost for establishing and running a monitoring committee is less than US$2,000 per year, which is mostly spent on telephone calls, internet usage, travel to meetings, food and beverages at meetings and some stationary. Compared to the total value of projects that are monitored by the focal points and monitoring committees, this is a highly effective operational cost. For instance, in 2011, the value of infrastructure projects that Luta Hamutuk and the community monitored was US$1,249,499 (see Table 1). In contrast, total monitoring costs for Luta Hamutuk in the same year was only US$1,677.30.

In addition to benefitting local people in Timor Leste, Luta Hamutuk has also been able to share and transfer the knowledge it has gained to its peers in similar post-conflict reconstruction contexts, thus indicating the potential for replicating its community-driven monitoring approach. For example, the model of the monitoring committees has been adopted by Integrity Watch Afghanistan (a partner of Integrity Action, and a member of the Networking for Integrity in Reconstruction).

Compared to other approaches that have been carried out by other international agencies in Timor Leste, this community-driven monitoring approach is considered successful. For example, a European Union evaluation report states that based on the evaluator's interviews with community members, government and other key stakeholders, all of them were 'expressing great satisfaction' with Luta Hamutuk interventions related to improving their awareness about the national budget, revenues and spending, as well as the quality and implementation of public infrastructure project.[14]

Most development interventions focused on provision of inputs and services, such as agricultural inputs for production to farmers, construction of schools and health clinics for communities and so on. Communities are usually not involved in monitoring projects or

---

14 *Report on the evaluation of the East Timor national CSO, Luta Hamutuk, for the period of July 2005-July 2008, page 17.*

services because this is seen as too technical for them. In contrast, Luta Hamutuk builds local capacity for monitoring through its training programmes for focal points, as well as its emphasis on empowering local communities to be active citizens.

Another community-driven development programme that was implemented on quite a massive scale in Timor Leste was the World Bank's Community Empowerment Program (CEP), with a total budget of US$18 million for a five-year project, which was concluded in 2004. Modelled on a community-driven development programme predecessor in Indonesia known as Kecamatan Development Program (KDP) – a sub-district development programme with an emphasis on transparency and accountability – it relied on the already popular idea for promoters of good governance in the international community (Moxham, 2005: 523). KDP focused on community participation at the local level (Olken, 2007: 205) and, similarly, the CEP team also aimed at improving transparency, accountability and local participation as the project's expected outcome. CEP meant to distribute development funds for poverty alleviation directly to the local communities through local councils on a nationwide basis that were organised by local facilitators hired by the World Bank. CEP funded a range of community projects, such as road repair, water sanitation projects and microcredit-funded kiosks (Moxham, 2005: 523). The thesis was that by facilitating communities to participate in managing their own development projects, local communities would be empowered (Independent Evaluation Group, 2011: 50-51).

The difference between Luta Hamutuk's approach and the World Bank's CEP approach can be seen in two main issues: first, the commitment to put local resources first in resolving issues and to build local capacities; and second, the commitment to reinforce existing structures and accountability mechanisms.

Putting local resources first. This is epitomised in the presence of the focal points as part of the local community themselves rather than hiring outsiders as facilitators. The focal points have proven to be more effective than the CEP facilitators because their commitment and dedication to their respective community is stronger. Moreover, use of focal points does not involve too much cost, since they work on a voluntary basis. The Luta Hamutuk approach also stresses the importance of capacity building and processes to increase community awareness by providing knowledge. In contrast, because its emphasis is on disbursement of CEP infrastructure project budgets, those community members who were involved were pressurised to spend funds on projects within set timeframes that did not allow enough time to increase local capacity. As a result, the local communities saw the project merely as a source of income, and not in terms of improving social capital, as stated in CEP objectives.

Commitment to reinforce existing structures and accountability mechanisms

As indicated above, monitoring committees are multi-stakeholder forums with the aim of working to support and ensure the account-ability of public infrastructure projects. To achieve this, monitoring committees engage with various government offices, as well as par-ticipate in Luta Hamutuk's advocacy initiatives. In contrast, the lo-cal councils established through the World Bank CEP project 'were introduced on the contradictory premises that they would not only fill a governance void at the local level but also provide clarity to the complex structures already in place' (Moxham, 2005: 24). This attempt was considered unsuccessful because it appeared to not just ignore local governments, but also the traditional leaders and clandestine resistance networks that previously existed. Other gov-ernment agencies that Luta Hamutuk also works closely with are the parliament, especially the Infrastructure and Financial Com-mission, the function of which is to oversee the executive budget proposal and the related executive arms of the government: infra-structure, public works, finance, health, education and gender (Sec-retary of State for the Promotion of Equality).

In particular, the Luta Hamutuk approach ensures that commu-nity-driven accountability mechanisms work in complementarity with existing state institutions and accountability mechanisms that are responsible for preventing corruption, such as CAC. CAC is a quasi governmental body the main function of which is to acceler-ate anti-corruption education, prevention and investigation. Since 2009, it manages and implements the anti-corruption work that used to fall under the jurisdiction of the Anti-Corruption Division of the Ombudsman for Human Rights.

Aside from serving as the legal framework that brings corrupt actors to court and expedites the handling of their cases, CAC also emphasises the importance of preventive action and public awareness. Luta Hamutuk shares similar political will with CAC in terms of enhancing public awareness to prevent corruption: Luta Hamutuk works at the district, sub-district and village level to promote transparency and accountability through monitoring, whilst CAC works at the national level.[15]

The relationship between Luta Hamutuk and CAC first began when anti-corruption efforts were still held by the Ombudsman for Human Rights Office. After CAC was established, the relationship continued, whereby Luta Hamutuk supports CAC by providing evidence and data, but does not get involved in the litigation process (such as hearings, court appearances, etc.). In particular, two cases were followed up as a result of cooperation between Luta Hamutuk and CAC. The first was a case of mismanagement and corruption by the head of the Los Palos Hospital, who gave his brother and his wife a government project to procure health facilities and equipment. CAC was successful in bringing a case against the hospital head on the grounds that his actions constituted a criminal abuse of authority. The second case was also about the criminal abuse of authority, with the same hospital head found guilty of borrowing money from his wife and paying her back with government funds. In both cases, Luta Hamutuk provided data and relevant documents about these instances of fraud to CAC, and CAC followed it up.

Despite government rhetoric to support anti-corruption efforts, as a formal institution CAC is still weak. Community members and Luta Hamutuk can find and report corruption cases, but if the role of CAC is not strengthened and reinforced, no legal action can be taken to bring corruptors to court. In fact, the number of real cases that have gone to court is low, especially when related to anything to do with top officials. Between 2009, when it was officially set up, and January 2012, for example, CAC has investigated and brought to court only 30 cases. The lack of supporting legislation

---

15 *It is expected that sometime in late 2012 Luta Hamutuk and CAC will sign a memorandum of understanding (MoU) as a legal basis for their both parties to cooperate. The draft MoU has already by approved by Luta Hamutuk and sent to CAC for review. If there are no changes or modifications to the draft, the MoU will be finalised and signed by both parties.*

and rules, such as a mandate to arrest perpetrators of corruption or do wiretapping to collect evidence against them, along with the absence of a special court for corruption cases, further weakens this anti-corruption agency. CAC likewise lacks adequate resources: its professional human resources are insufficient for the large-scale task it faces, as is its annual budget. CAC also does not have a network that extends down to grassroots levels. Yet it is at the grassroots level where first-hand information about corruption can be discovered, which is especially relevant for infrastructure development projects. CAC therefore needs and relies on support from Luta Hamutuk to reach local communities and coordinate work at these lower levels.

Challenges

The community-driven accountability work that Luta Hamutuk has developed and undertakes is beset by a range of challenges:

- **Replication of Luta Hamutuk initiatives.** This is hampered by geographical difficulties in reaching some remote areas because of the poor infrastructure (eg, roads are barely passable). Equally challenging is the low level of education of the population in general, which makes it difficult for local residents to understand the materials provided.
- **Low participation of women.** Budget and oil transparency issues are seen as 'masculine' issues, so it is difficult to get women to participate. Luta Hamutuk has attempted to encourage women to participate by engaging with women's groups and NGOs such as Redo Feto, Alola Foundation, Fokupers, Caucus, etc. In addition, women are disproportionately affected by low levels of education, which can affect their self confidence to appear and speak in public, including at community meetings.
- **The domination of local authorities.** Within the monitoring committees, local government representatives tend to dominate proceedings, which might serve to reduce a committee's capacity for criticism during monitoring and advocacy. Briefings and meetings can serve to build the capacity of other committee members so that they can be more assertive in voicing their concerns during committee meetings.

- **Working with media has its shortcomings.** The restricted geographical coverage of the media throughout the country limits the outreach effect of these channels of communication and advocacy. Low literacy rates also hinder access to mass media, like newspapers, factsheets and even village announcement boards. Low income levels may prevent people from purchasing printed media or electronic media devices; eg, television or radio.
- **Weak parliament.** Members of parliament do not have the capacity to perform their oversight role. They often do not have the technical skills needed to perform their duties. Because they seldom meet constituents outside of election times, they do not fully understand community concerns and therefore cannot really represent them. This lack of parliamentary oversight capacity increases the burdens of Luta Hamutuk's community-driven accountability work.

Conclusions

Empowering local communities to participate in a community-driven monitoring approach builds a more solid foundation for a sense of citizenship among local community residents who are generally marginalised from the issues and decision-making processes that affect their daily lives. This approach also promotes good governance, especially on infrastructure construction projects. Importantly, this approach is more sustainable because of the primary role that local communities play. Its cost effectiveness can guarantee that community-driven monitoring continues, even after international NGOs and donors withdraw. The success and effectiveness of this community-driven approach is evidenced in the recent interest that the Asian Development Bank (ADB) has shown in adopting it for its own infrastructure project in Timor Leste.

In establishing this community-driven monitoring approach, Luta Hamutuk plays more of a bridging and facilitation role that is focused on the process. An essential part of this work is to build local monitoring capacities, which also ensures that local communities are more independent of external supports.

Recommendations

1. More people should be encouraged to participate in this community-driven accountability approach, especially those who are marginalised and excluded because of their social and economic status, including women. Illiterate people (who make up almost half of the total population) are those who must be encouraged to participate in community briefings. Luta Hamutuk can use an array of participatory tools for this end, in particular those that involve more drawings and pictorial illustrations, rather than written texts.
2. Community-driven accountability mechanisms should also take into account the oversight role of parliament with respect to government projects, as they have a legal mandate to do so. If parliament lacks an effective oversight capacity, this should be strengthened.
3. It is important to network with donors and civil society organisations both to avoid the problem of duplication of efforts and to enable the scaling up of this approach. The inquiry from the ADB is a good start for efficiently replicating and scaling up Luta Hamutuk's community-driven approach. This also indicates that it would be beneficial for the organisation to engage with other local and international agencies to extend the reach of their approach.
4. In the long run, Luta Hamutuk could advocate for a formal accountability mechanism that requires public participation. This could also include, for instance, a policy demanding that each government infrastructure programme sets up its own complaint/grievance mechanism as part of the technical requirement of a project before it is implemented.

References

Bria, E. and A.K.N. Jorgensen. 'Local Solutions to Conflict and Corruption in Timor Leste' (unpublished Luta Hamutuk paper), 2011.
Independent Evaluation Group. Timor-Leste Country Program Evaluation, 2000-2010. Washington, DC: Independent Evaluation Group, the World Bank Group, 2011.

Luta Hamutuk. '2011 Annual Report'. Dili: Luta Hamutuk, no date.

Luta Hamutuk. '2010 Annual Report'. Dili: Luta Hamutuk, 2011.

Luta Hamutuk. 'Luta Hamutuk's Annual Reports: July-December 2009'. Dili: Luta Hamutuk, 2010a.

Luta Hamutuk. 'Luta Hamutuk's Six Monthly Report: January-June 2009'. Dili: Luta Hamutuk, 2010b.

Moxham, B. 'The World Bank's Land of Kiosks: Community Driven Development in Timor-Leste', Development in Practice, 15:3-4, 2005, 522-528.

Management Systems International. Corruption Assessment: Timor Leste (consultancy report). Washington DC: United States Agency International Development (USAID), 2009.

Olken, B.A. 'Monitoring Corruption: Evidence from a Field Experiment in Indonesia', Journal of Political Economy 15 (2), 2007, 200-249.

. . . .

Buy local, build Afghanistan: Building Markets

by Ainsley Butler

The final case study in this book again moves to a new theme: development. Aiming to increase the proportion of international spending in Afghanistan going to local business, Building Markets, a Canadian NGO, offers another strong example of a locally owned approach in action. It also represents the common sense that inspires Local First, especially in fostering self-reliance. To amplify local procurement capacities, Building Markets worked both on the demand side, making buyers aware of Afghan businesses and enabling them to distribute tenders, and on the supply side, helping Afghan businesses to meet buyers' standards. This case study best demonstrates the potential cost effectiveness of Local First, which seeks to have a broad economic impact rather than cost savings alone. Building Markets has now transferred responsibility for its key services to local partner organisations. The intensive training that accompanied this shift to a locally led approach achieves a primary objective of Local First: development initiatives should leave local organisations stronger and more capable than at the outset.

Local sourcing: a successful example

The international military forces in Afghanistan drink a significant amount of bottled water. Between 2001 and 2006, international forces imported all their bottled water into Afghanistan from neighbouring countries. The US military estimates having spent US$58 million on shipments of water in 2006 alone. The bulk of the costs were spent on transportation and shipping.

This presented a perfect opportunity for Building Markets, a non-profit organization that connects entrepreneurs in developing countries with new business opportunities. In recent years, investors had built modern bottling plants to provide safe and affordable drinking water in Afghanistan. These investments have provided hundreds of Afghans with access to jobs. One of the larger plants, Afghanistan Beverage Industries, employs over 350 workers. At the

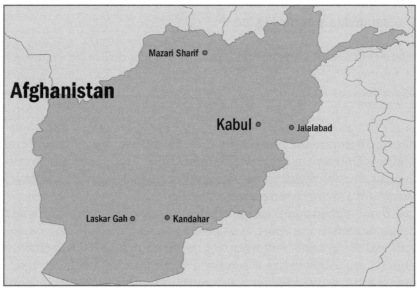

Map showing impact of project

US military's request, Building Markets conducted an initial assessment of the Afghan mineral water bottling sector. They identified and helped the US military team to visit 12 bottling factories.

In October 2006, the US military became the largest purchaser of Cristal water, produced by Afghanistan Beverage Industries. 'This is a landmark event,' said USMC Major David Van Bennekum. 'This is the first time an Afghan-based company has met the stringent standards placed on vendors providing food goods to US forces.' This represented significant savings for the US Military, as costs were reduced from US$58 million to US$7.2 million per year.[1]

Following the US military's lead, NATO's International Security Assistance Force (ISAF) also inspected and tested the Afghanistan Beverage Industries' plant and products. The first shipment of bottled water was received at ISAF headquarters in April 2007. Overall, buyers anticipated savings of over approximately US$2.8 million per year from buying this commodity locally. Local suppliers are expected to receive an estimated US$10 million from these contracts, generating a significant economic impact in Afghanistan.

---

1 Source: 'AFP, Coalition Buyer Local, Helps Bolster Afghan Economy', Middle East Times, 27 October 2006.

The importance of buying local

Since 2001, the international community has disbursed hundreds of billions of dollars for military, humanitarian and development operations in Afghanistan. This unprecedented level of spending has resulted in progress in terms of reconstruction and the restoration of critical services. Despite these successes, the complex security environment, along with high levels of unemployment and under-employment, has raised alarms about Afghanistan's uncertain future. Set against a backdrop of transition, including military withdrawal and reducing levels of international spending, many argue that a key to Afghanistan's future success lies in the continued development and support of its private sector.

Maximising the involvement of the local market in all activities underway in Afghanistan can contribute to broader economic development and reduce reliance on external support. Increased spending in key market sectors helps to 'spend the development dollar twice', using development and reconstruction monies to develop industries in the formal economy, which in turn creates local jobs, promotes stronger economic growth and increases government revenues. Spending funds on initiatives that have a local economic impact also benefits other sectors through the Keynesian multiplier effect, which refers to the number of times an additional dollar of fiscal stimulus cycles around the economy as a result of increased business activity. There has been a growing consensus that the business community in Afghanistan needs to focus on domestic market development, regional trade and the emerging extractive sector to lessen dependence on international aid and create an economic transition that is self-sustainable.

Building Markets implemented the Afghanistan Marketplace Initiative (originally known as the Peace Dividend Marketplace – Afghanistan) in order to increase the economic impact, and the resulting peace dividend, of the massive international military, aid and humanitarian presence in Afghanistan. This innovative approach built on the success of the Kabul Procurement Marketplace, a pilot project funded by Canadian International Development Agency (CIDA) from January 2006 to March 2008.[2] The project facilitated

2 *In a study about quantifying the local economic impact of peacekeeping operations that Building Markets conducted for the United Nations Department of Peacekeeping Opera-*

roughly US$60 million of spending in Afghanistan, far exceeding the initial target of US$5 million. Subsequently, the project expanded to other regions in Afghanistan with field offices in Mazar-e-Sharif, Jalalabad, Kandahar and Lashkar Gah, where funding from the UK Department for International Development (DfID) allowed for a fully-staffed office. The initiative was operational for six years, closing in March 2012 at the end of the funding agreement.

Building Markets relied on a team of Afghan staff. Local knowledge lies at the core of its project model, so the majority of staff were recruited from the local community. This was the best way to build trust with the local business community and ensure that the services offered are responsive to local needs. At project close, the team was comprised of 26 dedicated staff, who worked to ensure the delivery of project services.

Entrepreneurs are responsible for creating 86 per cent of new jobs in the developing world.[3] For this reason, the Marketplace initiative targeted Afghan small and medium enterprises (SMEs). In 2008, 80 per cent of local businesses that the project team worked with employed less than 50 people. Although the international community was not the intended beneficiary, the services also helped organisations contribute to stabilisation whilst making their procurement practices cheaper and more efficient.

Building Markets' experience in Afghanistan provides an important demonstration effect for local procurement.[4] Overall, the Afghanistan programme helped local businesses win contracts worth over US$1 billion, through which businesses reported they created

---

tions in 2006, the limited, yet significant, economic impact generated by the international presence in developing countries became obvious. Despite less than ten per cent of eight out of nine mission budgets being spent locally, the mission monies that did circulate within the economy had a significant effect on GDP and could help to kick-start a war-torn economy. Increasing local procurement of goods and services was identified as the best way to improve the economic impact of peace operations. The recommendations in this report that were made to ensure greater impact formed the basis of the Kabul Procurement Marketplace model, piloted in 2006. See: Michael Carnahan, et al. 'Economic Impact of Peacekeeping: Final Report', March 2006; http://buildingmarkets.org/sites/default/files/economic_impact_of_un_peacekeeping_march_2006.pdf.

3   The World Bank Development Research Group. Finance and Private Sector Development Team. April 2011. 'Small vs. Young Firms Across the World: Contribution to Employment, Job Creation, and Growth'.

4   Successful implementation of the project in Afghanistan led to expansion of the model to Timor-Leste (2007-2010), Haiti (2009-2012) and Liberia (2011-present), with plans for further expansion to two additional markets in Asia and Africa in 2013.

Local procurement is key to eradicating poverty

'International aid agency procurement has a role to play in the eradication of poverty, by providing capital investment through local and regional sourcing. By ensuring that supplier sourcing takes place in the countries and regions where the outcomes of the procurement function is to occur, procurement is able to influence:

- Job creation.
- Increases in income.
- Capacity in spend categories.
- Advances in economic opportunities within communities.
- Contribution toward economic development.'

Source: UN Procurement Practitioner's Handbook, November 2006.

---

or sustained 65,500 full-time equivalent jobs. This provides a grant effectiveness indicator of US$212 spent by donors per full-time equivalent job.[5]

The Sustainable Marketplace Initiative's services

Building Markets designed a suite of six inter-related services to increase the economic impact of the international community in the local economy whilst supporting local entrepreneurs by connecting them to new business opportunities. These were designed to address barriers on both the buyer and supplier sides. Buyers often lack reliable information about goods and services available in-country, and do not know how to effectively access the local marketplace.

On the suppliers' side, there is limited knowledge of tendering opportunities (and how to access tenders), of procurement procedures

---

5 *In an effort to better understand and measure the impact of the project, DfID asked Building Markets to engage the services of KPMG LLP to provide limited assurance over three key performance indicators: 1) number of contracts facilitated; 2) value of contracts awarded; and 3) number of jobs created through project interventions. KPMG LLP undertook an evaluation of Building Markets' methodologies, data collection processes and reported data, whilst also conducting a review of information related to attribution/ counterfactual; ie., confirming how Building Markets can capture attribution data in the future. A limited assurance engagement was conducted by KPMG LLP in 2012 to verify data collected by Building Markets. The assurance report is included in the project's final report. See Ainsley Butler, et al. 'Impact Report: Afghanistan Marketplace Initiative 2006-2012'; www.buildingmarkets.org/our_impact.*

and of contractual matters. In addition, both buyers and suppliers are hampered by asymmetric information about the marketplace. Addressing the information gap faced by all stakeholders is a key component to develop domestic business capacity and maximise the economic impact of the international presence in Afghanistan.

Training

Targeted training seminars were provided to local suppliers in order to increase their understanding of procurement processes and enable them to successfully bid for, and win, contracts. Additional training modules in project management, business accounting, sales and marketing and proposal writing were provided in the last half-year of the programme based on local business requests.

From 2006 to 2012, the team trained employees from 1,556 businesses. Nearly half of suppliers (47 per cent) reported that they had integrated all course elements into their business and 64 per cent reported participation in more tendering opportunities. To some extent, suppliers attributed feedback related to 333 contracts worth US$144 million to their participation in the training sessions.

The training service was a valuable source of capacity development within the Afghan marketplace according to 87 per cent of survey respondents who reported having received no other training. The Deputy Commander and Principal Assistant Responsible for Contracting – Afghanistan underscored the utility of the training services by stating that Building Markets had 'organised numerous contractor training sessions, vendor days, and a first ever Women's Owned Business Conference in order to promote contractor capabilities and economic growth… each of these important events… have been extremely successful'.[6]

Tender Distribution Service (TDS)

This service collected tender announcements and other business opportunities and distributed them to local companies. To reach the maximum number of businesses, information was disseminated online in the tender directory (www.afghanistan.buildingmarkets. org/tenders), by email, or by short message service (SMS). Hard

---

6 *Letter to Building Markets from Jeffrey D. Willey, Colonel, United States Deputy Commander and Principal Assistant Responsible for Contracting – Afghanistan, Bagram Air Field, 29 April 2009.*

copies of tenders were distributed through the Marketplace offices to reach companies that did not have internet access.

TDS was intended to increase suppliers' access to, and awareness of, contracting opportunities. Many buyers operating in Afghanistan only publish procurement opportunities on their own websites. A recent audit of Afghan First initiatives found that buyers did not consistently use the same methods to announce opportunities, thereby reducing the visibility and accessibility of tenders available to Afghan businesses. Without the ability to find tenders, suppliers stand little chance of being able to bid on and/or win contracts.

In an effort to support suppliers, the online tender directory was developed and launched in the summer of 2010. The TDS team conducted daily research, using over 126 different sources (websites, newspapers, etc.) in order to consolidate opportunities on the online tender directory. Prior to this, a weekly notification of open tenders was sent to suppliers, who could pick up the tender documents at programme offices. In total, 7,530 tenders were circulated through the TDS. Suppliers won 527 contracts worth US$190 million through access to the TDS.

Business Matchmaking
Business Matchmaking connected buyers looking for goods and services with verified local businesses who could meet their requirements. This was done by various methods, such as providing custom reports of local providers, promoting market linkages, making site visits, and organising vendor events and networking opportunities that were attended by both buyers and suppliers.

The intent of this service was to turn buyer requests into contracts for local suppliers. In Afghanistan, examples of these activities included the first-ever Female Business Leaders conference and other specialised conferences, site visits to small-scale manufacturers, information sessions and supplier-buyer events. Memoranda of Understanding with buyers such as the US military and UNDP helped to ensure that international organisations made use of services to access local suppliers.

Online Supplier Directory and business verification
The Online Supplier Directory provided buyers with information on local businesses. The directory featured business profiles that

Women's networking events

In 2011, the Afghan Women First Business Matchmaking event was hosted in Kabul. The goal was raise the profile of women-owned businesses in Afghanistan to show members of the procurement community that capable local women-owned companies were able to provide goods and services in high-impact sectors.

Seventy representatives from diverse sectors, including logistics, construction, media, textiles and furniture supply, attended the event. Buyers included representatives from the US military, UN agencies and several key Afghan government ministries. One female supplier, who specialises in media and marketing consulting, said of the event, 'It's a great opportunity to meet the important buyers we otherwise don't have access to.'

Building Markets polled the participating suppliers the day of the event, and all of them indicated that they had made connections to buyers and other organisations with investment opportunities. Six weeks later, three contracts worth over US$55,000 were awarded.

Buyers also changed their procurement processes after the event. Some buyers decided to email these women-owned businesses directly about new business opportunities, others built databases of women-owned businesses to better track and utilise those vendors, and still others set aside contracts specifically for Afghan women-owned businesses.

include information related to the company's contact information, organisation and structure, qualifications and licensing, range of operations and past performance. Accessible through the Afghanistan Business Portal, the directory could be searched by sector and location. Marketplace staff initially verified each supplier profiled in the directory through on-site, in-person interviews. Businesses were re-verified by telephone every six months to maintain the integrity and the utility of the data.

The Online Supplier Directory is intended to increase access to reliable information on the local market for buyers and suppliers. Such information is scarce in Afghanistan and this directory addressed a gap in knowledge about local businesses, particularly in areas where procurement officers are unable to meet suppliers face-to-face due to security restrictions. The importance of the directory is highlighted in a report from the Special Inspector General for Afghanistan Reconstruction (SIGAR) published in January 2012, which states, 'Of the databases used by contracting authorities, only the [Building Markets] database provides information on a prospective awardee's sufficiency of resources.'[7]

Since May 2008, the homepage on the Afghanistan Business Portal has received over 905,000 site visits from 334,231 unique visitors, resulting in more than three million page views. Sixty-one per cent of all visitors to the Portal were returning visitors.

For many organisations, the Online Supplier Directory became an important operational resource, and it received tens of thousands of site visits each month. For example, the Principal Assistant Responsible for Contracting in Afghanistan (PARC-A) requested that Building Markets provide access to the directory in a Memorandum of Understanding that was signed in March 2008:

> '[Building Markets is] to provide PARC-A and RCCs online access to its business listing that includes recently vetted firms and other information [Building Markets] decides to include to improve the opportunities for increasing business with competent and emerging Afghan firms.'

Call centre

The in-house call centre was the backbone of data collection systems. Call centre staff contacted all of the businesses registered on the Online Supplier Directory every six months, updating information and removing businesses if they had closed down. Every three months the call centre also undertook impact surveys for training and TDS services. These surveys took place over the phone and respondents were asked a series of questions about the impact of Building Markets' services.

Market information and advocacy

This activity generated data and reports that contributed to a fuller

---

7   *Special Inspector General for Afghanistan Reconstruction (SIGAR), 'Afghan First Initiative Has Placed Work with Afghan Companies, but is Affected by Inconsistent Contract Solicitation and Vetting, and Employment Data is Limited', page 9, 31 January 2012; http://www.sigar.mil/pdf/audits/2012-01-31audit-12-06.pdf.*

A note on gender

Gender equality in the workplace and in all activities that were undertaken within the Sustainable Marketplace Initiative was a key component of the project. In order to better understand the role of women at work in Afghanistan, activity-specific, gender-disaggregated data on female entrepreneurship, female employment and women-owned businesses was collected wherever possible.

Women-owned businesses won 65 contracts valued at over US$56 million. The Afghanistan Supplier Directory listed 272 women-owned businesses, which were operating in ten different geographic regions and across 22 sectors. Of 142 capacity building workshops that were conducted for Afghan businesses, 100 female participants representing 90 women-owned businesses received training. This accounted for 33 per cent of all women-owned businesses listed in the supplier directory.

All activities conducted by the project contained a gender focus that supported female entrepreneurship. Training sessions, networking and outreach events, exclusively for female entrepreneurs, were conducted and co-hosted. These events were designed not only to build capacity but also to provide female entrepreneurs with networking opportunities and allow them to share successes, lessons learned and new business opportunities.

From May 2008 to March 2012, ten events and vendor days for female entrepreneurs and women-owned businesses in Afghanistan were held. These events were attended by 300 female participants representing 270 Afghan women-owned businesses.

---

understanding of the impact of local procurement in Afghanistan.[8]

In general, the market reports found that after using the available services, buyers found it easier to access local suppliers. Local suppliers increased their confidence and developed skills required to work with large buyers. The aim to change market behaviour over time was met as buyers were increasingly able to rely on the local market, and suppliers became better at competing for contracts.

Additionally, local businesses were able to create jobs in

---

8 *To read these reports, see: http://www.buildingmarkets.org/our-impact/afghanistan.*

Afghan women-owned businesses win manufacturing contracts

In 2008, Building Markets put together a Female Business Leaders Conference for women-owned businesses. This event led one buyer to announce in 2009 that they wanted to set aside a portion of their textile-manufacturing contract for a woman-owned Afghan company. The buyer's contracting body approached Building Markets to identify companies that would be eligible to bid. A dozen women-owned companies were identified and received the tender.

The first rounds of bids were not up to standard, but the contracting agency realised that the common deficiencies in the proposals stemmed from a lack of understanding about the bidding process. The buyer decided to put the contract up for a second time.

In order to improve the quality of bids, several pre-performance seminars where businesswomen could meet the contracting officers and have the bid explained to them in detail were organised. Over 60 participants from 35 different companies attended these. In addition, samples of equipment were distributed to bidding companies so that they could ensure that they were making the same quality of produce for their sample submission. Smaller companies that could collaborate specifically for this bid were also linked up. In the end, dozens of high-quality bids were submitted.

The first round of contracts were all awarded to Building Markets-sourced suppliers, either as a unique company or a joint venture. Three companies won two separate groups of contracts that have a base year initial purchase of US$54.3 million total. The total contract ceiling on the option years is over a billion dollars.

One of the winning companies credits Building Markets as being instrumental in winning the bid. Building Markets alerted them to the project, provided them with samples and helped connect them with another company to create a joint venture. The company CEO said, 'As women, it is not always easy to operate in the private sector because most business happens through old networks which we never had access to in the past. This will give us an opportunity to get on our feet to be a bigger player in the business community. We are grateful to [Building Markets] for encouraging Afghan women entrepreneurs and we hope they have more programmes for women in the future.'

Afghanistan, since labour was required to deliver on contracts. Businesses used profits to invest in physical and human capital, thereby increasing their ability to deliver more contracts in the future. Businesses were able to grow and acquire a track record of successful contract completion, which inspired more investment and confidence in the local market.

Achieving impact

The services described above are designed to increase the amount of money international buyers spend through local suppliers. In locations where local suppliers would likely be engaged by buyers due to a lack of options (eg, in field offices) these services contribute to increasing the pool of local suppliers receiving contracts, which creates a more diversified and sustainable marketplace.

Each service offered contributes to increasing local procurement and its impact. Overall, buyers find it easier to access local suppliers, whilst local suppliers increase their confidence and develop skills required to work with large buyers. The aim is to change market behaviour as buyers are able to increasingly rely on the local market whilst suppliers become better at competing for contracts.

When local businesses win contracts, labour inputs are required to deliver on those contracts, thus creating and sustaining local jobs. Businesses use profits to invest in physical and human capital, thereby increasing their ability to deliver more contracts in the future. Businesses are able to grow and acquire a track record of successful contract completion, inspiring more investment and confidence in the local market.

Building Markets: theory of change

- Market-driven economic growth is a critical factor to eradicate poverty. Over the last 20 years, more people have been lifted out of extreme poverty, measured either relatively or absolutely, than at any time in history. This progress was due, in large part, to the growth of SMEs.
- The fastest and most effective way to grow SMEs is to give them access to

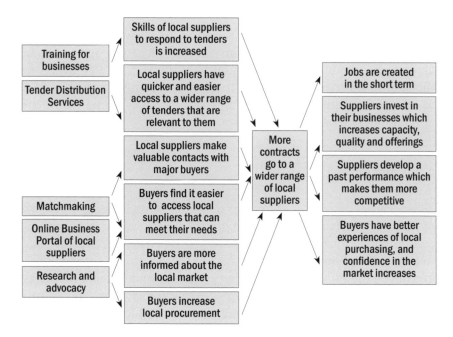

Figure 1: Linking each service to expected outcomes and impact

new markets. There is very little developed economies can teach local entrepreneurs who operate in countries that have endured conflict or natural disaster. They already know how to provide competitive goods and services. What they lack is access to larger international buyers.

- The easiest markets to access are the ones that are already there. In places like Afghanistan, Mozambique or Liberia, there are two economies that coexist in the same country, but rarely interact. International agencies and multinationals spend billions on these economies, but not in them. Goods and services get flown in because in many cases it is easier to call a dealer in Dubai than walk down to the local market. This disconnect is 'low hanging fruit': an opportunity to create more efficient markets by linking pre-existing supply and demand.
- Barriers in these markets are due to asymmetrical information. Buyers cannot find sellers; sellers don't know how to find buyers. Local entrepreneurs do not necessarily need new equipment or better management systems. They only need to know where to find

Graph 1: Total value of contracts

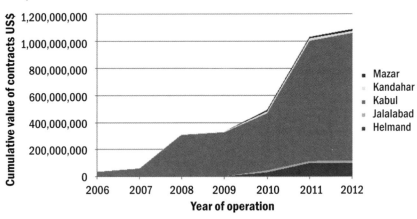

international tenders, and how to understand and bid on them. Similarly, international buyers do not need subsidies to buy local. They just need more and better local bids.

- **Connected once, local sellers no longer need assistance.** They can find the next contract on their own. Once a local entrepreneur gets help to win an international contract, they do not need it again. Crucially, their competitors see and learn, and soon they too are bidding and winning international contracts. Unlike other types of developmental assistance, this change is self-sustaining and does not need ongoing third party assistance. The Sustainable Marketplace Initiative makes local SMEs more sustainable, it does not seek to make the intervention itself sustainable.

Quantifying impact: the demonstration effect

In total, 1,364 contracts valued at US$1 billion were recorded from feedback from buyers and suppliers in Afghanistan from January 2006 to February 2012, where help from Building Markets' services was a factor in securing these contracts. In Helmand, from January 2009 to February 2012, 349 contracts were recorded, valued at over US$100 million. This impact registered on the scale of the national economy. In 2008, awarded contracts were 2 per cent of Afghanistan's GDP; in 2009, 0.32 per cent; and in 2010, 1 per cent.

The contracts won with the help of programme services

Chart 1: Comparison of contract volumes

Year	Value of contracts won with the help of Building Markets' services US$	Value of US contracts awarded to Afghan companies US$	Value of contracts awarded to Afghan companies by three UN agencies US$
2008	247,969,298	121,543,636*	50,235,424**
2009	22,668,281	236,374,137*	55,329,338***
2010	159,334,416	378,729,394*	80,714,724****

*As reported through the FPDS, **UNOPS and UNDP, ***UNOPS, UNDP and UNICEF, ****UNOPS and UNICEF. Sources: UNOPS: http://www.unops.org/ english/whatweneed/Pages/Contractawards.aspx. UNDP: http://www.undp.org.af/ Operations/Procurement/contracts.htm. UNICEF:http://www.unicef.org/search/search. php?querystring=contracts%20awarded&hits=10&type=Main. US contracts: Analysis of data from US Federal Procurement Data System, using Afghanistan vendor code only (www.fpds.gov).*

also represent a significant proportion of local spending from international buyers operating in Afghanistan. The table above shows publicly available data on spending from three UN agencies and US government entities from 2008 to 2010.

Jobs created and sustained

Employment is one of the most important impacts of contracts awarded to Afghan businesses. Creating jobs in crisis and post-crisis countries is fundamental to reducing poverty and rebuilding fragile economies. It is also considered crucial for stability. Whilst there are many ways to support private sector growth, sourcing goods and services where possible is an efficient way to jump-start an economy and set off a multiplier effect that leads to job creation.

Over six years, Afghan businesses were helped to create or sustain an estimated 130,000 six-month jobs, or 65,000 full-time equivalent jobs. On average, businesses increased staff size by just under 200 per cent during contract periods to meet the demands of the contract.[9] The majority of these new hires were skilled workers and

---

9 *Smaller businesses experienced a higher percentage of employee growth. This might indicate that smaller firms had a less steady supply of contracts and were therefore less able to retain a permanent core team.*

almost all were employed for the duration of the contract.

Since these jobs are strongly linked to contracts, the continuation of local procurement should be at the heart of any development strategy or government programming in future, since it helps the private sector to add jobs and generates taxable revenue for government. Limiting local procurement is likely to result in the loss of jobs within Afghanistan during the transition period and afterwards.

In November 2011, information was collected from a small number of employees on the importance of their jobs. The income from these jobs is desperately needed; more than half of the respondents were not able to save any of their salary. Those that were able to save did so for their family, their education or the future. Family and education were the two biggest categories of expenditure. This focus on education is a positive sign in a country where skilled workers are in short supply.

As well as earning money, employees gained skills and experience. General business experience and working in a team were the two most common things employees reported learning at work, followed by finance experience.

Sustainability and local partners

The goal of Building Markets is not to have its own projects be sustainable, but rather to help make local businesses more sustainable. By helping businesses become more robust, the aim is to build the economies of developing nations, reducing their dependence on aid and making them more resilient.

Due to persistent and ongoing demand, the tender distribution service was transferred to local partner organisations. In Kabul, the Afghanistan Chamber of Commerce and Industries (ACCI) was selected due to the complementary nature of their mandate and presence across many provinces. Established in 1931, the ACCI is an independent organisation that serves the advocacy and business facilitation needs of the private sector. Its mandate is to promote trade and investment by opening new markets for Afghan products and matching potential buyers with potential sellers. ACCI membership represents approximately 90 per cent of the total Afghan workforce. Headquartered in Kabul, the organisation operates in 21 out of 34 provinces. Its current membership is composed of 37,000 private sector organisations, including 25 sector-based business associations. A strong entrepreneurial culture underpins ACCI's work, which will help facilitate the transfer of the training and tender distribution service.

The Helmand National Investment Association (HNIA) was selected as the other partner. The HNIA was formed in October 2010 to serve the advocacy and business facilitation needs of members of the Afghan private sector in Helmand province. A majority of the businesses in Helmand trade as sole or small enterprises, and there was a clear need for a representative association. The HNIA's mission is to support local businesses, encourage investment and foster economic growth and employment in Helmand. In particular, the Association plays a prominent role in providing investors with an access point to the Helmand marketplace. The Association links international demand to local supply, providing a practical, effective and sustainable pillar of private sector growth and job creation in the province.

Staff from these two local partner organisations received intensive training on both activities for a period of approximately six months. This training culminated in a final evaluation that was administered to partner staff as a competency test to ensure that all of the concepts had been sufficiently understood in order for them to autonomously take over management of these services.

Challenges

Collecting feedback from buyers and suppliers
Building Markets established successful working relationships with buyers and suppliers alike. However, obtaining information from buyers on local procurement transactions was consistently difficult. This is due in part to the fact that some buyers are understaffed, and therefore do not have the time to collate contract confirmation. Turnover rates are high within buyer organisations and can be as frequent as every three months, creating difficulties in maintaining the institutional memory required to confirm attribution of transactions to a specific project service.

Suppliers were generally amenable to providing information on the contracts they were awarded, but sometimes hesitant to give out detailed information for fear of retribution from competitors, that the information would be reported to the government or make them a target for criminality. Some companies do not keep standard business records, and therefore could not provide accurate information.

Managing remote relationships with buyers and stakeholders in regions

With the closure of the field offices in Mazar-e-Sharif, Jalalabad and Kandahar in 2010 because donor funds had ended as planned, it was a challenge to maintain relationships with buyers and stakeholders remotely. Buyer relationships are often personality driven and contracting officers are frequently rotated in and out. The success of the field offices was largely dependent upon building strong relationships with stakeholders on the ground. Without a standing presence in the provinces, there was a noticeable drop in matchmaking requests received from regional centres.

Security context

Afghanistan's security environment made it challenging to conduct surveys. Businesses are often hesitant to provide details, especially specific details such as contract reference numbers, to an outside organisation – even one with significant local staff. Some mentioned that they feared the information they provided would fall into the hands of tax collectors who might choose to tax them unfairly. Others revealed that sharing details about their involvement in international contracting might make them vulnerable to retribution or violence for supporting the international presence in Afghanistan.

Fee for service

In early 2011, it was agreed with the project donors, DfID and CIDA, to try and wean local beneficiaries off donor dependency for the delivery of certain free services. The idea was to move toward fees-for-selected-services in the autumn and/winter of 2011-2012. Research surveys of beneficiaries were conducted in the spring of 2011, which revealed a high degree of willingness to pay fees for selected services: specifically Afs 5,000 (US$100) for an annual subscription for the tender distribution service; and Afs 4,500 (US$90) for a participant's attendance at each of the three half-day workshops entitled Introduction to International Procurements.

When pilot-testing of the fee-for-service approach was introduced in Helmand during October 2011 and then in Kabul during November 2011, the rate of positive responses by targeted clients (all of whom had responded positively in the spring) turned out in fact to be almost zero. In future, it may be necessary to charge fees for training from the start of an intervention.

Monitoring and evaluation

This initiative was evaluated twice by independent consultants. The first evaluation, in January 2008, concluded that the early pilot project had achieved its outputs and outcomes, as well as exceeded its goals. A second evaluation was conducted in August 2010, which noted that the main challenge facing the project was the definition of a clear exit strategy, including handover to local organisations.[10]

Grant effectiveness
A grant effectiveness indicator was developed for this project that represented the average donor funds spent from May 2008 to March 2012 per job generated by suppliers that were supported by the Afghanistan Marketplace programme. This indicator provides a high-level view of the effectiveness of funds disbursed by both DfID and CIDA. DfID's contribution can be correlated to the creation of 14,866 six-month jobs at the cost of £90 (US$145) per job, or 7,433 full-time equivalent jobs at the cost of £180 (US$290). CIDA's contribution can be correlated to the creation of 107,618 jobs, with spending at CA$108 (US$109) per job.

Overall, funds from both donors contributed to the creation of an estimated 131,006 six-month jobs, costing US$113 per job or 65,503 full-time equivalent jobs at the cost of US$226.

Sustainability of SMEs
A key challenge as the international community scales down in Afghanistan is the question of sustainability of Afghan SMEs. With the withdrawal of the US military, the Afghan private sector will have to shift its dependence on military spending and reposition itself to respond to more local and regional demand. Increasing

---

10 *See footnote 2 above for more detail.*

Kick-starting manufacturing: boots for the Afghan National Army and the Afghan National Policy, a short-lived success story

Building Markets first verified the Melli Company in 2006. The company was a well-known footwear manufacturer before the civil war. During the civil war, the Taliban looted the factory and the family fled to Pakistan. Fifteen years later, after returning to Kabul, the company operated its trading company with ten to 15 staff.

In 2007, the US military approached Building Markets to inquire about footwear products that could be sourced in Afghanistan. Through its business matchmaking service, Building Markets introduced Melli to the US military's Contracting Center in Kabul, and a contract was subsequently awarded.

The opportunity led to a decision at Melli to invest US$6 million in purchasing new machinery and increasing production capacity. In addition, Melli went on to hire 250 full-time employees. The US military awarded Melli a Blank Purchase Agreement (BPA) in September 2007 for footwear. The US military often uses BPAs to order and pay for supplies and services that are purchased from approved vendors several times a year, simplifying their processes.

A few months later, Building Markets arranged a factory site visit with US military contracting officers. During this visit, the contracting officers were able to meet with and provide valuable feedback to Melli's management. The officers explained that Melli's quality control mechanisms had been substandard, as a result of which Melli had not been awarded subsequent contracts. Melli's management was keen to make the necessary improvements in order to meet US military standards and win additional contracts. Subsequently, the company was awarded a trial contract for manufacturing 2,000 boots. Melli was able to successfully complete this contract to the desired product specifications.

When the US military again sought locally manufactured boots, Melli was awarded a sole-source contract because it was deemed the only company in Afghanistan with a fully operational boot-making factory. After a nine-month research and contracting process, Melli was awarded a contract valued at over US$87 million. To complete the contracts, Melli employed 700 Afghan shift staff. >>

>> Fast forward to 2012. Farhad Safi, the company's chief executive, indicated to The New York Times that Melli has received no new boot orders for eight months. He said, 'As the international coalition withdraws and Afghanistan is forced to pay more for its own equipment, the government [has turned to] buying Chinese and Pakistan boots – which are lower in quality but cost 15 per cent less.'

Although a 15 per cent discount on boots may appear significant, the loss of 700 jobs for Afghans due to a lack of demand has a significant negative impact on the economy.

Source: Graham Bowley, 'Afghans Fear Downturn As Foreigners Withdraw', The New York Times, 31 January 2012.

the capacity of local SMEs is vital to the longevity and success of Afghanistan's fledgling entrepreneurs. Connecting these businesses to other regional opportunities, as well as attracting increased levels of foreign direct investment, will ease the transition. To do this, however, Afghan entrepreneurs must be credible and confident enough to attract international investors. As US military operations and the broader international presence winds down, support for the local private sector should not.

Conclusion

International buyers are increasingly turning to Afghan entrepreneurs, driving job creation and GDP growth. Due to this support, the growing importance of the domestic private sector in reconstruction and other economic opportunities will play an increasingly positive role in stabilising Afghanistan. As international spending draws down, or shifts towards the extractive industries and other forms of foreign direct investment, the Government of Afghanistan's procurement needs will provide an opportunity to further support the national economy.

One strategy could be for the Afghan government to start its own 'Afghan First' programme, taking stock of lessons learned and building on past experience. Since entrepreneurs are responsible for generating 86 per cent of jobs in the developing world, this would be a policy position worth examining.

Recommendations

The following are key recommendations learned from the Sustainable Marketplace Initiative in Afghanistan. These recommendations are intended to help guide future efforts to include the SME sector at the heart of development in Afghanistan.

Government of Afghanistan

- Take a leadership role in developing and implementing local procurement regulations that support the loval private sector.
- Continue to improve the business enabling environment in Afghanistan, including improving Afghanistan's doing business ranking.
- Champion Afghan First approaches to humanitarian, development and reconstruction initiatives.

Afghan private sector

- Work in partnership with the Government of Afghanistan and the international community to ensure that Afghan SMEs are supported through the transition period and beyond.
- Diligently improve business standards, customer service and transparency and attention to detail.
- Re-invest profits in business modernisation.
- Be prepared to pay for business development and professional services.
- Train and develop human resources in procurement practices in Afghanistan.
- Provide internship opportunities to students to acquire business skills.

Good practices for the international donor community

- Require all contractors and implementing partners, wherever practical and cost-effective, to procure goods and services locally for project work before sourcing offshore.
- Prioritise Afghan companies in procurement processes,

particularly those dealing in locally produced goods.

- Share information about planned expenditures earlier so that the business community can be more responsive to demand.
- Publish local procurement policies.
- Consistently post tenders online at www.kabul-tenders.org and www.helmand-tenders.org and other sites, so that businesses can always access tenders.
- Measure economic impact and job creation effects as part of regular programme implementation.
- Whilst properly adhering to their procurement regulations when determining if the local vendor meets their 'capital adequacy requirements', development partners should assess, in that determination, prevailing local criteria such as 'credit line' rather than solely 'funds in bank'.
- Reduce the size of contracts so that small companies can bid
- Simplify procurement documentation and forms.
- Improve terms of payment (ie, on-time payment).
- Contribute to efforts to build qualified, local vendor lists.
- Provide training to local suppliers on procurement protocols.

· ·

End note

The 'help for self-help' slogan in development assistance discourses already carried the seeds of what has now turned into a fully-fledged controversy: the question about whether outside interveners or local stakeholders should be shaping the process that eventually leads fragile countries to economic progress, institutional change and stable peace. In essence, this is a debate about how to improve existing practices, which is still sorely needed.

Whilst this battle over local ownership in transition processes has somewhat subsided in the field of development assistance and statebuilding, it still rages within the peacebuilding community. On the one hand, there are those who favour the liberal peace model, arguing that peacebuilding in post conflict countries is an effort 'to bring war-shattered states into conformity with the international system's prevailing standards of domestic governance' (Paris, 2002: 638). According to proponents of liberal peace, existing universal norms surrounding the principles of good governance are the gold standard of peacebuilding which must be followed at all times and in all places (Bush, 1996: 86). As a corollary of this universal claim, local actors have little room for manoeuvre to define this process and their role is basically reduced to implementing predetermined Western world solutions.

On the other hand, those who oppose this liberal peace model favour what is generally termed a communitarian approach, or peacebuilding from below. As Ken Bush summarises this perspective, 'The challenge of rebuilding war-torn societies is to nurture and create the political, economic and social space within which indigenous actors can identify, develop, and employ the resources necessary to build a peaceful, just, and prosperous society' (*ibid*). Rather than relying on a universal template, communitarians stress that sustained solutions to the problems of political order and good governance must originate within the society itself and take into account country-specific traditions. Moreover, local actors must actively be engaged and empowered to act on a self-reliant basis so as to avoid the dependence scenario.

At first glance, Local First seems to provide a simplistic answer to the liberal peace versus communitarian debate. Undoubtedly,

Carolyn Hayman is a strong advocate of the communitarian model when she writes, 'Local First is a development approach that looks first for the capacity within countries, before bringing in external expertise and human resources, and which recognises that much of this capacity is found outside central government' (see the Introduction). Many applaud her, since this position obviously reflects a good deal of common sense. Others argue that Local First is naïve, mainly because certain implicit assumptions about this approach can be viewed as problematic.

First, there is no such thing as one local perspective. It is a reality that societies in fragile states in general and in post-conflict countries in particular are deeply divided. Hence, the notion of local ownership, which tends to assume a minimum of social cohesion and commonality of purpose among local actors, is rarely present. There is, as Timothy Donais observes, never a 'single set of local owners... since peacebuilding is a highly politicized process in which one does not only have to accommodate the diverging interests of local and external actors but also forge domestic consensus around fundamental political issues' (Donais, 2009: 11-12). Thus, whilst 'abstract notions of local ownership enjoy wide acceptance in principle, such notions offer little concrete guidance in determining whose voices should be prioritized among the cacophony of local owners' (*ibid*: 12). Dan Smith concludes that 'a failure to recognize the reality of the conflict context might make a simple commitment to local ownership almost fatal to the hopes of successful peacebuilding' (Smith, 2004: 26). Surely, then, the idea of local ownership is complex.

Second, the communitarian vision of local ownership assumes that local owners will possess the capability, the capacity and the will to pool their efforts towards the creation of a just, stable social and political order. Although the local actors presented in the case studies exhibit them, these qualities are clearly not universally available. Whilst there are always pockets of such competence to varying degrees, this assumption is nonetheless questionable. In West Africa and in Central Asia – regions I am most familiar with – the capacity of local intellectual elites to structure comprehensive peace processes is usually limited, and the few outstanding civil society representatives are often involved in a wide range of political and economic activities which, in the end, can seriously impede their effectiveness and efficiency. The political elites, too, can represent a dubious set of local owners. Once elected or co-opted to power, they all too often go astray and embark on criminal or near-criminal behavior.[1] Instead of taking on an ownership role of the peacebuilding process and committing themselves to build an inclusive, democratic, and economically prosperous society, they frequently use their positions to enrich themselves.[2]

There are other potential pitfalls that challenge both the communitarian and the liberal peace vision of peacebuilding, like donor dependency, the politicised realities of conflict, situations that paralyse civil society actors, etc. The Local First approach neither ignores these challenges, nor does it stumble on the impediments outlined above. For Local First does not mean a 'local only' approach, as in the absence of necessary capacities and capabilities it allows external experts to contribute to getting the job done. Thus Local First is not at all dogmatic; in fact, it is very flexible. Perhaps this is its greatest strength: pragmatic in(ter)vention.

As the case studies in this book show, in order to be successful, peacebuilding requires that all available resources are mobilised – both local and international, governmental and civil society actors, business and non-profit enterprises alike. An entrepreneurial combination of external intervention and local efforts is needed, with concerted attention from the outset to finding, growing and nurturing local capacities. What counts is to do the right things at the right time and to empower capacities for peace, wherever they are found. At the same time, it is necessary to dismantle structures that hinder progress towards building a functioning state which abides by the rule of law and puts in place the mechanisms needed to cope with conflict in a constructive, nonviolent manner.

The pragmatic stance of 'Local First – Outsiders Second' does

---

1 *This does not only hold true for members of political parties but, as the case of the transitional government in Guinea has shown in 2010-2011, for political leaders emerging from civil society as well. As soon as the representatives of civil society had gained power and had the opportunity to realise personal economic gains, a majority among them could not withstand the temptation. Some local interlocutors even argued that corruption and embezzlement of public money were considerably higher during the interim government under Jean-Marie Doré than previously. It is of course impossible to verify such accusations, but it is striking that members of the interim government who before their nomination had no significant financial resources at all, are equipped with expensive four-wheel-drive cars and living in neat villas after only one year in office.*
2 *See Donais, 2009: 32-33.*

not solve all the problems that lie at the heart of peacebuilding. On the contrary, what in theory sounds nothing less than logical entails in reality many tough questions. Who defines whether capacities are in place to the extent which is needed? And which capacities are we talking about, to do what? Capacities needed to build a democratic state or capacities to build a state that is predominantly based on traditional forms of statehood? Do we want, for example, to reinforce a judicial system imposed on a state during colonial times? Or do we want to resurrect a pre-colonial system that, in the meantime, may have been completely discredited through the ruthless practices of corrupt governments? Or are there entirely different options that move beyond such stark choices? Above all, who is the 'we' making these decisions? Depending on how these questions are answered, external support and resources are either needed or not. Effective peacebuilding thus requires difficult decisions about whether certain structures should be empowered or dismantled. Are, for example, authority structures based on clientelism a vital source of social capital, or an obstacle to the establishment of modern political institutions?

The Local First approach does not give easy answers to these questions, and the many dilemmas which peacebuilding communities around the globe face remain in place. The discussion, however, makes it evident that the communitarianism versus liberalism debate should no longer be framed in either/or terms. Instead, we should attempt to find the middle ground between local and outside solutions for the best possible combination of available resources. We should also be aware that this is always going to be a very difficult task – precisely because that ground is constantly shifting and changing; precisely because the people who stand on that ground constitute a diversity of capacities, experiences and interests. As a corollary to this insight, we also need to acknowledge that there are no one-size-fits-all solutions. Depending on the history and the socio-cultural-political context, strategies about how to create viable states that manage to provide security and economic prosperity for their people vary from case to case. At the same time, we should be modest and humble about what can and cannot be achieved within the inevitably complex, politically volatile and dynamic contexts of any peacebuilding effort.

The transition from the Millennium Development Goals to

the post-Busan New Deal that will define how the international community engages with fragile and post-conflict states provides an opportune moment to re-think the role of local stakeholders and the valuable expertise therein. Seeking to improve business as usual in the fields of peacebuilding and state-building, Local First recognises all this and more.

Heinz Krummenacher, Bern, 12 September 2012

REFERENCES

Paris, R. 'International Peacebuilding and the "Mission Civilisatrice" ', Review of International Studies, 28:4, 2002.

Bush, K. 'Beyond Bungee Cord Humanitarianism: Towards a Developmental Agenda for Peacebuilding', Canadian Journal of Development Studies Special Issue, 1996.

Donais, T. 'Empowerment or Imposition? Dilemmas of Local Ownership in Post-Conflict', Peace & Change, Vol. 34, No. 1, January 2009.

Smith, D. 'Towards a Strategic Framework for Peacebuilding: Getting Their Act Together', Overview Report of the Joint Utstein Study of Peacebuilding. Oslo: Royal Norwegian Ministry of Foreign Affairs, 2004. See: www.dep.no/filarkiv/210673/rapp104.pdf.

APPENDIX 1: AUTHOR PROFILES

NASTASIA BACH was a short-term intern at International Bridges for Justice (IBJ) for four months in 2012. She completed a degree in International Relations at the University of Southern California in 2010 with an emphasis in international security and international political economy. Nastasia will begin a law degree at the School of Oriental and African Studies (SOAS) at the University of London this year and will work towards becoming a barrister. She is interested in human rights and criminal law, and especially the transitional justice process in Cambodia.

AINSLEY BUTLER is Chief Investment Officer at Building Markets. Previously, she was the organisation's Project Director and Senior Advisor for Afghanistan and Haiti. Ainsley's field work includes an appointment as Building Markets Afghanistan Country Director and sustainable development consultant for a large-scale development project in Kandahar. Other work commitments have taken her to Haiti, Sierra Leone, Liberia, Kosovo, Timor Leste and Myanmar. She has also contributed to research related to aid effectiveness, development economics and the non-profit sector for the Government of Afghanistan, the Government of Canada, NATO and the OECD. She first joined Building Markets in 2005, focusing on the Economic Impact of Peacekeeping, a study commissioned by the United Nations. Ainsley has a master's degree from the Institut d'Etudes Politiques de Paris (Sciences-Po) and was a visiting graduate fellow at New York University.

VICTORIA FANGGIDAE is a Programme and Research Manager at Prakarsa, a national research and policy analysis institution based in Jakarta, Indonesia. Prior to this, she worked as programme staff for a number of international development agencies in Indonesia, such as Oxfam UK, United Nations Population Fund (UNFPA) and the World Food Programme (WFP). She also has engaged in various short-term projects as a consultant and researcher for the International Labor Organization (ILO) in West Timor and the Global Poverty Project (GPP) in Melbourne. As a West Timorese, Victoria is familiar with the context of the Timor Leste conflict. Her previous work with the WFP in East Timorese refugee camps in West Timor border towns reinforced and deepened this understanding. Recently, with Prakarsa, she has assessed and provided capacity building in policy analysis to Luta Hamutuk's staff and focal points in Dili. Victoria has a master's degree in Development Studies from the University of Melbourne.

KATE FLOWER *joined International Bridges for Justice (IBJ) as the Criminal Justice Project Officer in August 2011. She graduated from the Australian National University in 2006 and in 2007 was admitted to the Supreme Court of New South Wales. While completing her studies, and subsequently joining a private practice, Kate worked on a number of social justice programmes, including an Australian Senate Inquiry, drafting an ACT Legal Aid publication, and providing pro-bono services in two Community Legal Education Centres in both Australia and the UK. Prior to joining IBJ, Kate spent seven months volunteering at a community centre in one of the poorest slum areas of Siem Reap, Cambodia. Kate is also currently studying her master of laws at the University of Sydney.*

CAROLYN HAYMAN *is a co-founder of Peace Direct, where she has been Chief Executive since 2004. After a double First at Cambridge, and a Masters in Development Economics at SOAS, she joined the UK's Ministry of Overseas Development, and subsequently became a member of the Cabinet Office Think Tank at 26, working on many cross cutting topics, including the social impact of microelectronics. She took her knowledge of the emerging field of office automation into consultancy and then, as Joint Managing Director of the Korda Seed Capital Fund, into technology start-ups. In 1996 she moved to the Foyer Federation, a newly established network of projects providing accommodation and education for homeless young people. During this time she was also a Board member of the Commonwealth Development Corporation. In 2000 she joined the Network for Social Change, and in 2002 she began working with Scilla Elworthy to launch Peace Direct, which funds and promotes local peacebuilding in conflict areas.*

MAIRÉAD HEFFRON *is Programme Manager of the Digital Repository of Ireland, at the Royal Irish Academy. Prior to this, she worked in Mozambique for the United Nations Development Programme (UNDP) and as an independent consultant in the areas of crisis prevention and environmental issues. She has conducted research and contributed to various reports and publications on development issues, ranging from environmental rights to examining the use of ICTs in social movements. As part of a grassroots security sector reform initiative by FOMICRES, a local peacebuilding organisation based in Mozambique, she has conducted a project evaluation. She currently resides in her home country of Ireland. Mairéad has a master's degree in Development Studies from Kimmage Development Studies Centre in Dublin and a bachelor's of science degree in physics from Dublin City University.*

JESSICA KNOWLES *interned with International Bridges for Justice (IBJ-Cambodia) during the summer of 2012. She graduated from the Medill School of Journalism at Northwestern University in 2009 and moved to the Philippines soon after to research the treatment of child prisoners on a Fulbright grant. In 2010 she was selected for a Princeton in Asia Fellowship and spent the next two years working for human rights organisations in Timor Leste and Cambodia. Jessica is currently pursuing a JD at the University of Washington and a master of studies in International Human Rights Law at Oxford University.*

HEINZ KRUMMENACHER *is a Director and Head of Finance and Communications at swisspeace. Prior to joining the directorate in 2001, he was head of the swisspeace early warning programme, FAST International (1998-2008). Previously, Heinz was head of the social research and media department at IHA-GfK, a leading market research institute in Switzerland (1992-1998). Between 1990 and 1992, he served as foreign editor with the Swiss daily newspaper Der Bund. He began his professional career with the Swiss Defence Department, where he directed a study group dealing with the re-definition of Swiss security policy (1985-1989). In addition to his role at swisspeace, he is the CEO of the BEFORE project. Heinz has a master's degree and a doctorate in political science from the University of Zurich.*

KATE MCGUINNESS *is a consultant with extensive experience in editing, writing, fundraising and philanthropy, with an emphasis on peace and conflict related projects, as well as a range of topics linked to good governance issues. She is a founding director of Fox McGuinness GbR, a bespoke English language/German-English translation firm based in Berlin. She is also a member of the board of directors of Peace Direct's*

German affiliate. With co-author Victor Angelo, her latest publication is 'Security and Stability: Reflections on the Impact of South Sudan on Regional Political Dynamics' for the Norwegian Institute of International Affairs (NUPI). On behalf of the BEFORE Project, she also secured a grant from the UN Democracy Fund for a judicial reform project in Guinea. She has edited a range of publications for Democracy Reporting International. Prior to this, she was a senior advisor for the Berghof Foundation. Kate has a doctorate in Peace Studies from the University of Bradford.

HANS ROUW currently works as a Programme Leader at the Security and Disarmament Department of IKV Pax Christi, the largest peace organisation in the Netherlands. He has done extensive research in eastern Democratic Republic of Congo, Colombia, South Sudan and Nepal on the interaction between disarmament and community security and conflict transformation. He has additional research interests and programme management experience related to the topics of protection of civilians in military interventions, bottom-up approaches to security promotion and the prevention and reduction of armed violence. Hans has a master's degree in Conflict Studies and Human Rights from the University of Utrecht, with a focus on bottom-up conflict transformation and the interface between insiders and outsiders in conflict transformation.

RENS WILLEMS is finalising his doctoral dissertation at the Centre for Conflict Studies (CCS) at Utrecht University in the Netherlands. His research examines the ways in which international efforts to build or contribute to security in the hybrid political context of post-settlement countries relate to national and local perceptions and practices of security. A particular focus has been on disarmament, demobilisation and reintegration (DDR), security sector reform (SSR), armed violence reduction (AVR), and small arms and light weapons (SALW) control. He has done extensive field research in Burundi, eastern DR Congo and South Sudan, working closely with civil society and community-based organisations, as well as with policy-makers.

· ·

APPENDIX 2: ORGANISATIONAL PROFILES

Local First is supported by the organisations below, all of whom assisted in the creation of this book. We would be delighted to hear from other organisations and individuals interested in helping Local First or knowing more about it. For details and contacts, please see www.localfirst.org.uk.

BUILDING MARKETS *(formerly known as the Peace Dividend Trust) is a non-profit social enterprise that builds markets, creates jobs and sustains peace in developing countries by championing local entrepreneurs and connecting them to new business opportunities. Its flagship initiative, the Sustainable Marketplace, provides a suite of services proven to catalyse growth and to create, restore and sustain livelihoods. To date, these projects have redirected over US$1 billion into developing economies. In 2010, Building Markets was recognised as one of a handful of social enterprises affecting measurable and sustainable change in the developing world with a Skoll Award for Social Entrepreneurship. Building Markets also won the G20 SME Finance Challenge Prize for its Factor Finance for Procurement innovation. Launched in 2004 and headquartered in the US, Building Markets also has offices in Afghanistan, Canada, Haiti, Liberia and Timor Leste. Website www. buildingmarkets.org.*

CEDAC The Centre d'Encadrement et de Développement des Anciens Combattants is a non-partisan organisation aiming to support former soldiers to reintegrate socio-economically through training, peacebuilding and development projects, human rights promotion and grassroots community initiatives. To date, CEDAC has assisted with the socio-economic reintegration of 25,000 ex-combatants across the country. The organisation has also campaigned for the voluntary handover of firearms, monitored start-up business initiatives organised by ex-combatants, provided training in conflict prevention and management, facilitated peacebuilding activities for female ex-combatants, conducted lobbying and advocacy work, and engaged in a range of community development projects. Founded in 2005 in Bujumbura, CEDAC has ten staff members, a national network of active volunteer members throughout the entire country and representatives in other countries around the world. Website www.cedac.webs.com.

CENTRE RÉSOLUTION CONFLITS Based in eastern Democratic Republic of Congo, the part of the country most vulnerable to violence, for the past ten years the Centre Résolution Conflits (CRC) has been tireless in its work to rescue child soldiers, keep communities together, build relationships and train people from different tribes to live together peacefully. CRC directly deals with militia groups in the area, focusing on disarmament, demobilisation and reintegration. Although many militia members want to stop fighting, they are unable to see opportunities outside of the armed groups. CRC works with them in getting them to lay down their arms and integrate into the national army or find other means of income. CRC also works with refugees and internally displaced people, mediating between them and their former communities to assist their return. Website www.peacedirect.org.

FOMICRES The Força Moçambicana para Investigação de Crimes e Reinserção Social (FOMICRES) works towards achieving peace, social reintegration, reconciliation, development and crime prevention in Mozambique. It provides community training, advocacy and civic education so that community residents can identify sources of crime and violent conflict, and devise and implement locally based strategies to address them. Officially established as FOMICRES in 2007, the group of former child soldiers who founded the organisation first began working in 1995. Since then, FOMICRES has reintegrated over 1,000 child soldiers into their communities, collected and destroyed 850,000 artefacts of war, was the first civil society organisation to present to the UN on participatory DDR strategies, helped initiate HumaNet, a human security network in the SADC region, and was instrumental in establishing COPRECAL, Mozambique's commission on small arms. Website www.fomicres.org.

INTEGRITY ACTION (formerly known as Tiri) leads an active network of committed NGOs, universities and policy-makers working closely with governments, media organisations, businesses and their peers to identify way of making integrity work in some of the world's most challenging settings. Integrity Action was launched in 2003 and has offices in Jakarta, Jerusalem, London, Nairobi and Ramallah. The organisation is based on the conviction that integrity offers one of the largest opportunities for improvements in sustainable and equitable development. Integrity Action's mission is to empower citizens to act with and demand integrity, actively taking part in building institutions to promote a state that is open, accountable and responsive to their needs and expectations. Without integrity, measures to safeguard human rights, protect the environment, strengthen democracy, promote social equity and reduce poverty are compromised. Website www. integrityaction.org.

INTERNATIONAL BRIDGES TO JUSTICE (IBJ) is dedicated to protecting the basic legal rights of ordinary citizens in developing countries. Specifically, IBJ works to guarantee all citizens the right to competent legal representation, the right to be protected from cruel and unusual punishment and the right to a fair trial. IBJ works directly at the local level to train and employ lawyers to provide defence to indigent clients, as well as trains and empowers local justice officials most interested in achieving tangible reform. IBJ also builds international communities of conscience to support emerging legal aid organisations and advocates for the prioritisation of just and effective criminal justice systems. Founded in 2000 and headquartered in Geneva, IBJ works in Burundi, Cambodia, China, India, Rwanda, Singapore and Zimbabwe. Website www.ibj.org.

LUTA HAMUTUK (which means 'struggle together') is a local non-governmental organisation with over 150 community focal points across Timor Leste. Since the decades-long independence movement culminated in 2002, Luta Hamutuk has been engaging authorities in managing the nation's budget, natural resources and delivery of infrastructure and services. In this nation of just over 1.1 million, Luta Hamutuk connects the capital Dili, rural communities and international networks, including the Extractive Industries Transparency Initiative (EITI), bringing together government, civil society and the private sector at all levels. In addition to training and awareness raising activities at the community level, the organisation also plays an important advocacy role through its media campaigns. Officially established in 2005, the collaborative engagement and community monitoring facilitated by Luta Hamutuk has contributed to the delivery of critical infrastructure for more than 101,660 Timorese people. Website www.lutahamutuk.org.

PEACE DIRECT is an international agency that funds and promotes local peacebuilding in conflict areas. Peace Direct's goal is for local peacebuilding to be put at the heart of strategies for managing conflict. Currently it funds local peacebuilders in ten conflict areas in Africa and Asia and runs the website Insight On Conflict, an online showcase of local peacebuilding worldwide. As well as testing and developing Local First ideas in the field, Peace Direct seeks to influence those in the international community who can adopt Local First in their policies and practices. It has affiliate offices in the UK, USA and Germany. Website www.peacedirect.org.

SWISSPEACE *is a practice-oriented peace research institute seeking to promote the transfer of knowledge between researchers and practitioners. It conducts research on violent conflicts and their peaceful transformation. The organisation aims to build up Swiss and international organisations' civilian peacebuilding capacities by providing trainings, space for networking and opportunities for the exchange of experience. It also shapes political and academic discourses on peace-related policy issues at the national and international level through publications, workshops and conferences. The organisation focuses on a range of related research topics, including mediation, dealing with the past, gender, business and peace, statehood and conflict, and the analysis and impact of peacebuilding activities. Founded in 1988 to promote independent peace research in Switzerland, swisspeace now has more than 40 staff members. Website www.swisspeace.ch.*